# ROCKIN

| | |
|---|---|
| **SWEET HOME ALABAMA**<br>Second Helping | **SELF ESTEEM**<br>The Offspring |
| **MISTY MOUNTAIN HOP**<br>Led Zeppelin | **LONGVIEW**<br>Green Day |
| **BLACK BETTY**<br>Ram Jam | **MY NAME IS JONAS**<br>Weezer |
| **BREADFAN**<br>Budgie | **EMINENCE FRONT**<br>The Who |
| **PARANOID**<br>Black Sabbath | **COME AS YOU ARE**<br>Nirvana |
| **LA GRANGE**<br>ZZ Top | **CARRY ON WAYWARD SON**<br>Kansas |
| **19TH NERVOUS BREAKDOWN**<br>The Rolling Stones | **FORTUNATE SON**<br>Creedence Clearwater Revival |
| **FREAK SCENE**<br>Dinosaur Jr. | **MORE THAN A FEELING**<br>Boston |
| **MAYONAISE**<br>The Smashing Pumpkins | **PLUSH**<br>Stone Temple Pilots |
| **SURE SHOT**<br>Beastie Boys | **YOU REALLY GOT ME**<br>The Kinks |
| **DEBASER**<br>Pixies | **YOU SHOOK ME<br>ALL NIGHT LONG**<br>AC/DC |

*Dear Em,*

*Here's to many more books, burgers & the happiest of birthdays! I hope you have a wonderful day celebrating & that this book gives you many a culinary inspiration to creating the most epic burgers yet. Love Aggie xxx*

DJ BBQ

# THE
# BURGER
## BOOK

Banging burgers, sides and sauces
to cook indoors and out

**Photography by David Loftus**

*Hardie Grant*

QUADRILLE

# INTRODUCTION

**The cheeseburger! One of the most loved and eaten things in the Western world. It's the perfect meal to eat at home, on the road, in restaurants, at festivals or while hang gliding. Does anyone hang glide anymore? I should test that last theory...! Anyway, you can make them in various sizes and to different thicknesses. The world's your lobster when it comes to creating different types of burger. Heck, you can even make 'em out of lobster.**

The beautiful thing with a cheeseburger is that it can be held in the hand. Everyone loves to eat with their hands, and with burgers that's the norm. Forks and knives, be rid of thee! Run away cutlery! We don't need you anymore. We have a perfect food item that's delicious, juicy and easy to handle... apart from The King Burger (page 64). But that one should come with a warning. (In fact, please don't attempt The King Burger unless you plan on running a half-marathon or at least 10K the following day.)

Why am I doing a burger book? Well, my buddy T-Bone and I cook around 3,000 cheeseburgers every festival weekend. That's 20,000 a year. We love them and the people who frequent our food truck love them too. We've spent a couple of decades developing recipes for various burgers. The one we serve the most is in this book – it's the DJ BBQ Burger on page 71. Check out my previous book, *Fire Food*, for one of our other favourite burgers (The Ultimate Cheeseburger).

But this book has it all. Loads of delicious beefy burgers, and some more adventurous ideas. Remember, it doesn't have to be just beef to constitute a burger. It's got everything from chicken, fish and even just veg in a bun! Heck, sometimes I don't even use a bread roll. Wow, blasphemy!

This entire book can be cooked indoors or outdoors. It's all down to what you feel like doing on the day. Feel free to play around with the recipes. I am here to inspire and guide you on your burger journey. You are the burger chef and it's all about your freedom of expression. You might want a tangier sauce or maybe a more savoury vibe to your patty. Play with the ingredients and mix in your own ideas with ours. These recipes work. They are awesome! But I want you to have fun and be creative as well.

Take this book, put Tom Petty (RIP) on your Walkman, turn it up to a safe level and start making patties! Document your works of edible art, #theburgerbook and #djbbq, so I can share in your awesome triumphs.

Get cooking and rock out!

**Christian (DJ BBQ) Stevenson**

# THE ALCHEMY OF THE BURGER BUN

**Why is it that people are prepared to make their own beef patties but reluctant to bake the buns that go with them? Heck, I'm one of those people. That's why I went on a search for the best burger bun baker in the world.**

After a couple of years of trying out different types of bun, I finally found my bun nirvana – and it is not a place, it's a person. His name is David Wright, from the Cake Shop Bakery in Woodbridge, England. Dave recently won Best Baker at the Baking Industry Awards. It's the equivalent of winning an Oscar for baking. Dave has also won multiple awards for his brownies, including three stars at the Taste Awards. I know how hard it is to win three stars as I'm a judge for those exact awards! And, no, I sadly wasn't a judge when Dave submitted his brownies.

We use Dave's demi-brioche burger buns throughout the summer on the festival circuit. We normally order between 2,000 and 5,000 burger buns every weekend. Poor Dave – the man never sleeps. I contacted Dave to see if he could help with the book. I wanted to offer a burger bun recipe that any home cook could get to grips with – see page 10 for the recipe.

So, what constitutes the perfect burger bun? First, it needs to have a good structure so that it can hold all the lovely beef juices without falling apart. Second, even though the perfect bun is strong enough to hold all that goodness, you also need to be able to bite through it

without too much effort, so you can taste and chew the burger. You want those juices in your mouth, not your lap. (Okay, some juices might run down your arms but that's one super-duper juicy burger with loads of fat.) Third, the flavour of the bun needs to complement what's inside. The savoury goodness of a juicy cheeseburger needs to be offset by the buttery sweetness of a phenomenal bread bun.

Finally, a burger bun needs to look good as well. There should be a lovely shine to the bun, which is down to the egg glaze. This glaze is sometimes an after-thought. But let's look at it this way: if the beef patty is the engine, the bun is the bodywork. A muscle car with a beautiful clean glossy finish looks way better than a sports car with a matt finish or any car covered in dust. (Why would anyone have a matt finish on their car? I hate matt finishes. What were you thinking? So what if you are the top sales guy at the local estate agent, the matt black finish on your BMW looks naff!) Sorry, back to the burger bun.

In summary, a burger bun needs to be a combination of strong, soft, tasty and shiny in all the right places. On the following pages we've revealed the key steps to making the perfect bun.

## STEP 1: SELECTING THE RIGHT INGREDIENTS

You can't make a silk purse with a sow's ear. Dave said that – I had never heard the expression before, but I like it! It shall be mine. You'll need strong white bread flour, full-fat milk, yeast (fresh if you can get it, dried is okay), free-range eggs, caster (superfine) sugar, fine sea salt and butter.

## STEP 2: MIXING THE RIGHT INGREDIENTS IN THE PROPER WAY

If you add fat to the dough at the beginning, it will inhibit the development of the gluten, which is what provides the structure we need to hold the succulent juices of the burger. So, the butter goes in at the end after the dough has formed. When you add water to wheat flour, it introduces two proteins called glutenin and gliadin, which together form gluten. As the mixing process goes on, the gluten strands elongate and the structure of the dough improves. The journey of the dough is from porridge to parchment. Mixing is the key to making the perfect bun. But, if you mix too much, the structure of the dough degrades and becomes slack.

If this all sounds too technical, imagine a house party. The glutenin and gliadin get together to play some tunes and have a good time. They are dropping Prince, Madonna, Stevie Wonder and Michael

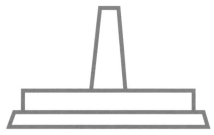

Jackson. To start off, it's just those two dudes (the proteins) in a room. As their protein buddies hear the music, they join the party. The room fills up to the point where you've hit the peak of your party vibes. This is when your bun dough is perfect. If you try and string the party out for too long, one by one everyone leaves and you've undone all your good work.

## STEP 3: FERMENTATION

During fermentation, flavours develop, structures improve and the quality of the dough is generally enhanced. You can compare fermentation with the process of dry-ageing beef. Chemical changes happen within the proteins in beef, as they start to break down after a couple weeks, which gives the beef a more dynamic flavour. Go too far, and the beef becomes quite cheesy, but if you hit it just right, the beef and fat has a lovely savoury/umami flavour and a great texture once cooked.

When you added the water to the flour back in Step 2, another process you initiated was the conversion of the starches to sugars. This is helped along by the enzyme called amylase. During fermentation, the yeast is then able to feed on the sugars, multiplying and releasing carbon dioxide. This carbon dioxide will fill the glutenous pockets you created during the mixing phase, causing the dough to rise.

## STEP 4: DIVIDING / SHAPING DOUGH

It's important that all the buns are roughly the same size. The beef patty shouldn't be hidden by the bun, nor should it poke out too far. The bun should frame the work of art that is your perfectly cooked burger. Getting the dough pieces as round as you can will help give your burger a great visual impact. Rounding dough balls can be quite difficult. The best way to get good at it is simply to practise.

## STEP 5: GLAZING

Giving that bun a lovely glossy look is all about the egg wash. The key to glazing is to brush the egg wash onto the dough ball before you let it prove.

## STEP 6: PROVING

During the proving process, the dough needs to rise again. This resurrection requires a specific environment. It needs both warmth and humidity. The warmth will encourage the yeast to metabolize at a speedy rate, releasing a fresh batch of carbon dioxide to inflate the dough balls. The humidity will keep the skin of the dough flexible, supple and malleable. If the skin of the dough dries out during this process, the dough ball would implode and nobody wants that. If you prove for too long, the dough ball might collapse as the yeast activity lessens. And if you don't prove for long enough, you'll get a dense, heavy burger bun. It's all about hitting the sweet spot with your timing.

So, to test the prove, you need to lightly touch the dough throughout the proving stage. At the beginning, the touch will result in an indentation in the dough that will take a while to spring back to its original form. At the peak of the proving process, the indentation from your finger should spring right back. And if you prove the dough too long, that indentation will remain and not spring back. If that happens, get it in the oven ASAP!

## STEP 7: BAKING!

The secret to getting the baking right is to take the dough at the peak time of proving and then hit it with exactly the right amount of heat. When that happens, your buns will expand rapidly. This is called 'oven spring'. Throughout the bake, the crumb (the middle bit) will set, the crust will caramelize and become glossy, and then they reach perfection!

## STEP 8: COOLING AND STORAGE

Allow the buns to fully cool down before cutting or storing. The butter needs to set. If you want to store your buns, make sure you use an airtight container so that they don't dry out. The burger buns will keep for at least three days.

# THE PERFECT BURGER BUN

## MAKES 15–20 BUNS

425g (15oz) strong white
  bread flour
10g (2 tsp) fine sea salt
50g (1¾oz) white caster
  (superfine) sugar
7g (1¾ tsp) dried yeast
15g (½oz/3 tsp) dried milk
  powder (optional but adding
  this will make your buns even
  softer – whoop!)
80ml (2¾fl oz/⅓ cup) warm water
75ml (2½fl oz/scant ⅓ cup) full-fat
  (whole) milk
4 eggs, beaten
175g (6oz) butter, softened
Vegetable oil, for greasing

## EGG WASH

4 egg yolks
50ml (1¾fl oz/scant ¼ cup)
  double (heavy) cream
Pinch of salt
Pinch of sugar

First, mix the flour, salt and sugar together in a large mixing bowl – this diffuses the furious battle that would commence should salt get its greedy hands on the yeast. Whisk the yeast and dried milk powder (if using) with the water, milk and eggs in a measuring jug. Pour the wet ingredients into the dry ones.

Knead the porridgey mess in the bowl until a dough forms. Turn the dough out onto your work surface and knead relentlessly while listening to AC/DC's 'TNT'. It will actually take you longer than that one song, so you could play the whole *It's a Shame About Ray* album by The Lemonheads – it's the perfect length for kneading dough. Or, you can do all of this in a bread mixer – way easier! But less fun.

Do the bubblegum test to see if your dough is on point. This involves taking a small piece of dough and gently stretching it as thinly as you can without breaking it. You should be able to almost see through it like a thin membrane on a maximally blown bubblegum bubble. Now we need to add the butter.

Cube by soft cube, add the butter into the dough while kneading. Your dough will become glossy and sleek. Lightly oil a large mixing bowl, place the dough in it and cover with a damp tea towel (dish towel). Leave in a warm place for 45–60 minutes until it has doubled in size.

Place the dough on a lightly floured work surface and divide into buns. You should get 15 to 20 buns out of this – weigh them out at 60–65g (2¼oz) a piece. Now you need to round these babies into perfect spheres. If you have OCD, please upload photos onto IG and tag #theburgerbook so we can share your beautiful work.

Now, mix that egg wash by combining the ingredients in a medium bowl. Line some baking sheets with baking (parchment) paper and place

all the dough balls on the sheets. Leave enough space between the balls as they will double in size. Completely coat the dough balls with the egg wash using a pastry brush. If you want to take this to the next level, you can do multiple coats, allowing a few minutes between applications. If you want to add any toppings, like sesame seeds, poppy seeds, pumpkin seeds, sunflower seeds, or even cheese (mmm...), then now is the time to dunk your buns. Dipping the balls is preferable to a light sprinkle, as the buns will expand during the prove and bake.

Don't forget to prove the dough before baking. It can take anywhere from 20–40 minutes. You can use your oven as a prover. Leave it turned off and put a baking sheet with a bowl of water on it at the bottom of the oven. Then put the buns in the oven and shut the door. The balls are ready to bake when you touch them gently and the indentation springs back quickly. This means the carbon dioxide is peaking and you are good to go. When they are ready to bake, take the buns out, and preheat the oven to 180°C (350°F/gas mark 4).

When the oven is ready, bake the buns for 15–20 minutes, until golden brown with a light brown colour on the base. Every single oven is different. Some are over-achievers and some are clunky pieces of junk. Your buns are ready when they are ready, so keep an eye on them but try not to open the oven – if you are lookin', you ain't cookin'! Well, you can look through the oven glass, just don't open the dang thing or your buns will be saggy.

Let the buns cool before slicing or storing them.

**TIP:** You can freeze the dough balls once you've shaped them into buns, and before you have glazed them. When you want to use them, just defrost, glaze, prove and bake as above.

# CUTS OF BEEF

The classic cuts used in beef mince (ground beef) for burgers usually come from the shoulder. Chuck is the most used beef for mince in the world, but different textures and flavours are good, so here is the DJ BBQ guide to the best cuts for burgers. If the cuts are dry-aged for a minimum of 21 days, then even better!

## 1 SHORT RIB

Huge fat content mixed with great bone flavour. The sweetest meat is next to the bone. The best burgers contain a percentage of short rib – it's got it all! As a cut, short rib only works when cooked slow and low. When you mince (grind) it, then it becomes some of the best meat for a burger you'll ever find. I can't enthuse about this cut enough.

## 2 BRISKET

Great marbling, awesome fat content and smooth flavour. Grain-fed brisket will always be fattier than grass-fed. The almighty brisket is one of the tougher muscles on the cow, but with that toughness comes great flavour. Brisket is a primal muscle from the lower part of a cow's chest. It is tough because it supports so much weight and a huge head – have you seen the size of a cow's head? Yeah, it's big.

## 3 CHUCK

Good all-rounder. Inexpensive with decent marbling: this cut could be used on its own. If you are pushed for time or are struggling to find specific cuts, then just go with this one – it works!

## 4 BAVETTE

Best flavour and excellent texture. Very lean. One of my favourite 'go-to' steaks. This is due to its incredible flavour. It just needs some fattiness to help it along. Hence, it's best mixed with fattier cuts or aged beef fat.

Other great cuts to use are flank, rib cap, Denver and, in some especially opulent cases, rib eye.

## 5 BONE MARROW

Bone marrow is the glorious river of succulence that every burger wants in its life. Every butcher will have this beautiful ingredient in abundance. Just ask at the counter. They normally take it from the leg bones and will cut the bones in half if you want. The reason marrow is so good is that its melting temperature is a lot lower than the meat cooking temperature, so it makes the burger really juicy while giving it a super-rich flavour! Wooooo! If you can't find bone marrow, then suet or aged beef fat are a great replacement. Some of the best burgers I've ever tasted have a very high percentage of aged beef fat.

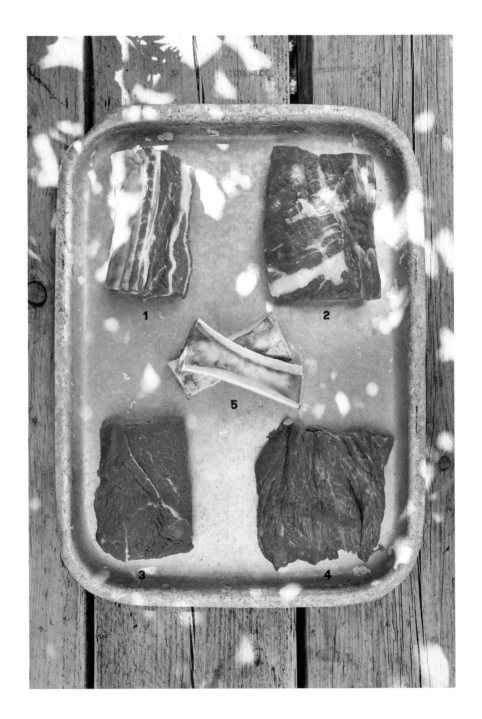

# GRILL SET UP

These techniques work for a classic kettle grill or similar. Just to be super clear, 'BBQ' is the food and not the grill. But people still call the grill the BBQ. What can you do?! In this book, I call it a grill or a cooker. I'm proper like that.

### HALF & HALF (INDIRECT VS DIRECT HEAT)

You'll cook the best burger if you have both indirect and direct heat on the grill. By this I mean one side of the cooker where there is no fuel heating the food above, and one side where this is fuel heating the food above. By having a direct side and an indirect side, you'll have more control over the heat your food is getting. Food will still cook on the indirect side, as there's always residual heat in the whole cooker. But it means you can move burgers from one side to the other to help you control the cook. This is called the Half & Half technique...

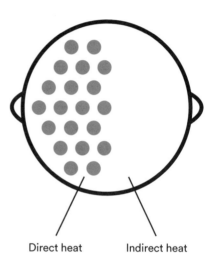

Direct heat       Indirect heat

Have the bottom and top pinwheels of your cooker fully open with this method. Get your coals cooking, lay them out over half of the base of your cooker. Leave one half of the base empty. This gives you a medium-hot heat over the coals and a large indirect zone where you can move food if things get too hot.

### DIRTY

This is a great way to roast garlic, potatoes, aubergines, onions and other vegetables directly in the coals. Add a solid bed of coals and get them cooking. Make sure that the coals are kept in a tight slab so they don't burn away too fast. Blow over the coals to dust away the ash just before you place anything on them. Then nestle your veg right in there.

## HOT SMOKER

This is a style of cooker, rather than a technique. It's great for cooking slow and low. It's designed for long cooks and allows you to top up fuel without opening the lid. You can still achieve great results on the classic kettle cooker, but it's just not as easy to control the heat for the long haul.

## TOPPING UP FUEL MID-COOK

Most of the recipes can be made using a kettle cooker (rather than a smoker), and most of them are pretty fast. However, if you do need to top up fuel, remember these tips:

- Add fuel every 50–70 minutes.

- If you're using quality lump wood charcoal, add a large handful of uncooked coals: about 8–10 coals

is ideal. You can use a chimney starter to pre-cook the coals and help maintain a constant heat in your cooker, but it's not essential.

- However! If you're using charcoal briquettes, you have to pre-cook them before topping up as the chemical binder used to make them can taint the taste of your food. Use a chimney starter for this.

# INTERNAL MEAT TEMPERATURES

**Knowing the temperature of your meat is one of the most important parts of cooking. Get yourself a temperature probe and your burger will always be cooked to perfection. Make sure you probe the thickest part of the meat and, if you do multiple probes, only use the lowest temperature you get.**

All the temperatures listed here are 'before resting'. Your meat will go up a couple of degrees during the resting phase.

If you can, always try and rest your meat in a warm place. Preferably not T-Bone's armpit. No one wants to go there.

If you know where your meat comes from and it isn't pre-packaged, you only want to cook in the rare to medium realm. It's all about the quality. The internal part of a piece of meat is free from bacteria, but the outside isn't. Therefore, it's important to source quality meat when going towards rare. If you aren't sure, then it's always safer to cook closer to well done.

## BEEF MINCE (GROUND BEEF)

| | |
|---|---|
| Rare | 54°C/129°F |
| Medium rare | 58°C/136°F |
| Medium | 60°C/140°F |
| Medium well | 65°C/149°F |
| Well done | 70°C/158°F |

## LAMB

You don't want lamb as rare as beef so I recommend the following:

| | |
|---|---|
| Medium | 55°C/131°F |
| Medium well | 60°C/140°F |
| Well done | 65°C/149°F |

## CHICKEN

| | |
|---|---|
| Minimum | 72°C/162°F |

## PORK MINCE

| | |
|---|---|
| Minimum | 72°C/162°F |

## FISH

| | |
|---|---|
| Minimum | 55°C/131°F |

## VEGETABLES

Temperature doesn't matter (although nobody wants a raw chip!).

# THE PERFECT BURGER BUILD

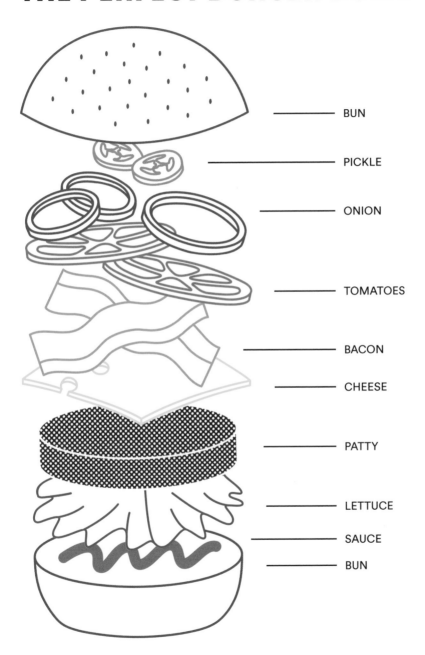

BUN

PICKLE

ONION

TOMATOES

BACON

CHEESE

PATTY

LETTUCE

SAUCE

BUN

# BREAKFAST
# BURGERS

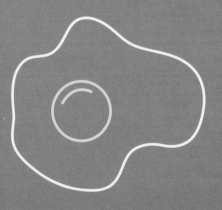

# BACON & CHEESE OMELETTE BAGEL

I used to live in Birmingham – the second biggest city in the UK and the birthplace of heavy metal. It's the home of Black Sabbath, Led Zeppelin and Judas Priest, while Thin Lizzy's Phil Lynott was actually born there. I was a disc jockey/host of the evening show at Kerrang! Radio from 7–10am every Monday to Thursday. My favourite on-the-go breakfast was this tasty concoction of utter greatness. I would knock it up in 7 minutes, jump on my skateboard and bomb hills to work while enjoying the tastiest bagel burger in the history of bagel burgers.

---

🔧 **MAKES 2 BURGERS**

🍖 **OUTDOORS** Half & half technique, with frying pan

▦ **INDOORS** Frying pan on the hob (stovetop)

---

4 smoked streaky bacon
  rashers (slices)
Knob of butter
3 eggs
Glug of cream or full-fat
  (whole) milk
50g (1¾oz) cheddar or Monterey
  Jack cheese, grated (shredded)
1 spring onion (scallion), sliced
2 bagels (best with onion or
  'everything' bagels)
Ketchup
Sea salt and black pepper

Heat up your frying pan – either over the direct heat on the grill, or a high heat on the hob – and get your bacon cooked. Make it nice and crispy for this recipe.

Remove the bacon onto some paper towel, then roughly chop. Leave the bacon fat in the pan so you can cook the omelette in all that awesomeness. (If you ain't digging that, you can wipe the pan clean and throw a knob of butter in instead.)

Half-beat the eggs in a mixing bowl, then add the glug of cream or milk and season with salt and pepper. Get your frying pan hot but not too hot (nothing worse than burnt eggs!) – either over a cooler part of the grill or over a medium heat on the hob.

Pour the eggs into the pan. Keep the egg moving with a fork until it's almost cooked. Then add the cheese, crispy bacon and spring onion. Fold, flip and cut into two.

Toast your bagels and place your omelette inside. Ketchup is good in the mix too.

# GET READY TO BLOW UP THE DEATH STAR BURGER

Luke Skywalker probably had this baby under his X-wing fighter seat as he took out the Death Star. Thanks Jyn Erso (Felicity Jones) for sacrificing your life so that others could live. (Hey, check out the movie I was in with Felicity, called *Chalet Girl*. It's a snowmantic comedy! You'll have to wait till the end to see my bits. I did get more lines than Brooke Shields though.) Sorry, back to the heroes of the story, Luke and this insanely delicious and filling breakfast burger.

---

✎ **MAKES 2 BURGERS**

🍴 **OUTDOORS** Half & half technique, with frying pan

📅 **INDOORS** Oven, plus frying pan and saucepan on the hob (stovetop)

---

2 medium potatoes (or 2 frozen hash browns, defrosted)
4 bacon rashers (slices)
Knob of butter
1 × 200g (7oz) can baked beans
2 eggs
2 crusty white rolls
Brown sauce

Preheat the oven to 180°C (350°F/gas mark 4) – or get a good bed of coals going. Bake your potatoes in the oven for 30 minutes until semi-cooked. Pull them out and let them cool. You could do this in advance, as they need to be totally cool before grating (shredding) and turning into hash browns.

While the potatoes are cooling, cook your bacon off in a frying pan either over the direct heat on the grill, or a high heat on the hob, then set it aside on paper towels.

Grate the cooled semi-baked potatoes onto a chopping board. Form two round patties that are a bit larger than the buns.

Get that bacon pan hot again, add a knob of butter to the bacon grease and cook the potato hash browns in the tasty fat (if you're using frozen hash browns, cook them now). Either way, don't flip till you got a good colour on the bottom. (My grandma always said, 'Don't be flipping your hash browns too much or they won't crisp up. They'll just be greasy and soggy.' Thank you, Grandma Stevenson.)

Dang, back to the destruction of the Death Star. Once you've achieved a lovely golden-brown crispy colour to the hash browns, set them aside on paper towels.

*Recipe continues...*

*Recipe continued from page 22.*

Crack open your can of baked beans and warm them up in a saucepan (over a low heat on the hob or over indirect heat on the grill).

Meanwhile, put your eggs into the frying pan and fry them off any way you like. For me, that's over easy with a runny middle. (Did you know that your body has a more difficult time digesting a firm yolk than a runny one? I learned that in Nutrition 101 at the University of Maryland. The dude who invented Google went there, as did Jim Henson.) Oh yeah, DEATH STAR! Nearly ready...

Stick your rolls in the fat in the frying pan and toast them off, then get ready to assemble.

Place the bottom roll on a plate and hit it with brown sauce for optimum coverage (or save it for the top), then spoon on the baked beans. Follow the beans with a hash brown each, then an egg, 2 slices of bacon and, finally, another squirt of brown sauce and the top of the roll.

Now, get in that X-wing and don't mess with gadgetry as you now possess the Force and a killer breakfast burger. Take out the Death Star! This recipe is dedicated to the memory of Jyn Erso as she died in pursuit of those essential Death Star plans. Pour a little bit of your morning coffee out in honour of Jyn.

# STEAK AND EGG BURGER

Nothing says breakfast better than steak and eggs... well, maybe a Full English, but let's not quibble. When we do outdoor events, this is the first thing we make to get guests' taste buds rocketing before we slam them with BBQ for eight hours! You could use any dry-aged steak for this but bavette towers above them all... especially when you pile 'em high like a tower.

---

✒ **MAKES 4 BURGERS**

🍴 **OUTDOORS** Half & half technique, with frying pan or plancha

🍳 **INDOORS** Frying pan and griddle pan (optional), on the hob (stovetop)

---

1 × 400g (14oz) dry-aged bavette steak, cut in half along the grain
4 eggs (8 if you are hungry)
Knob of butter
Chilli flakes (crushed chili pepper)
4 sourdough buns or 1 French stick
Dijon mustard
Sea salt and black pepper

First of all, make sure your steaks are at room temperature – leave them out of the fridge for at least an hour before you want to cook.

If you're cooking outdoors, you can cook your steak directly on the grill, or use a frying pan or plancha. If you're using one of those, get it nice and hot over the direct heat. If you're indoors, set your pan over a high heat on the hob.

Season your steaks with salt but no pepper. If you season with pepper at the beginning of the cook, the hot heat can burn the pepper and make the steak taste bitter and acrid. Save it for after!

Place the steaks into the pan or plancha or directly on the grill. Cook and flip, cook and flip. If your bavette is extra thick and you're cooking outside, you might need to move the steak to a cooler part of the grill or over the indirect heat so that the centre can catch up with the outside. Steaks are best served medium rare but take it where ya like it. Use a temperature probe to make sure the steak is perfectly cooked – check the internal meat temperatures on page 16.

When they're done, set the steaks aside to rest and crack over some black pepper. The steaks are still cooking and will take on the peppery goodness.

Now it's the turn of the eggs. Get your frying pan medium hot – either over a cooler part of the grill or over a medium heat on the hob – and add the knob of butter. Crack in the eggs, with a sprinkle of chilli flakes and salt, and fry them off just as you like them.

Toast your sourdough buns.

Slice the steak across the grain and season with
salt, then roll everything around so the resting
juices and salt cover every single bit of the sliced
steaky goodness. (Oh my god, I want to eat what
you are cooking right now! Can T-Bone and I come
over? I can't keep up with T-Bone's voracious
appetite – please feed him!) Next, layer up the
steak onto the toasted bottom bun with a dollop of
mustard. Top with the fried egg and the bun. Nice.

# MUSHROOM, SPINACH AND SOY TOMATO BURGER

My friend Ed has a theory: that mushrooms and spores came to earth via an asteroid. And since pigs and humans are the only species that eat mushrooms, then we must have come from space too. Anyway! This recipe was inspired by our friend and one of the best chefs on the planet, Manuel Scully. Scully loves to ferment and marinate his ingredients for super-duper triply long lengths of time. Which is amazing but we don't have the time as it's breakfast – 30 minutes will do. But, if you can, get those tomatoes marinating overnight, and you'll take this recipe to the side of the stage for a Guns N' Roses show during the Appetite for Destruction world tour.

 **MAKES 4 BURGERS**

🍴 **OUTDOORS** Half & half technique, with frying pan

🍳 **INDOORS** Oven, plus frying pan on the hob (stovetop)

2 tomatoes, sliced
50ml (1¾fl oz/scant ¼ cup) rice vinegar
100ml (3½fl oz/scant ½ cup) light soy sauce
40g (1½oz) brown sugar
1 spring onion, sliced
½ red chilli, sliced
Thumb ginger, peeled and sliced
Pinch each oregano, rosemary, and thyme, chopped
100g (3½oz) butter, softened, or 100ml (3½fl oz/½ cup) olive oil
4 portobello or field mushrooms (as big as your buns), stalks removed
Butter or oil, for frying
1 or 2 garlic cloves, sliced
1 chilli, sliced (deseeded if you like)
200g (7oz) spinach
4 brioche burger buns
Sea salt and black pepper

This baby needs a little prep. Marinate the sliced tomatoes in a bowl with the rice vinegar and soy sauce, sugar, onion, chilli and ginger for at least 30 minutes.

Mix the herbs with the butter or oil and spread over the top of the mushrooms. If you're cooking indoors, preheat the oven to 180°C (350°F/gas mark 4). Place the mushrooms on a baking sheet and roast for 10–15 minutes. If you're outdoors, cook them on your plancha or on the bars of the grill over the direct heat.

Meanwhile, stick a frying pan on a low heat on the hob (or over a less hot part of the grill) and a little butter or oil and lightly fry the garlic and chilli, until the garlic goes golden – a minute or so.

Now toss the spinach into the pan with a tablespoon of water. Throw a lid or baking sheet on top of the pan and sweat the spinach down. Stir a couple times. It won't take more than 2 or 3 minutes. Season with the salt and pepper.

When the mushrooms are cooked, get ready to assemble your veggie army of deliciousness. First, toast your buns. Place the mushroom onto the base of the bun. Top with the wilted spinach, a couple of slices of the soy tomato and the top of the bun. Carpe diem! Seize the day!

# THE DOUBLE EGG AND SAUSAGE McCHOPPY CHOP MUFFIN OR LOSE THE SAUSAGE TO GO VEGGIE!

I couldn't do a burger book without including one of T-Bone Chops's favourite breakfast behemoths. It may not look pretty, but it tastes beautiful!

---

🍴 **MAKES 1 BURGER**

🍖 **OUTDOORS** Half & half technique, with frying pan or plancha

🍳 **INDOORS** Frying pan on the hob (stovetop)

---

Vegetable oil, for frying
1 pork sausage, sliced lengthways
1 baked potato, sliced into flying-saucer rounds
2 eggs
2 slices of your fave cheese (burger cheese makes this more like a well-known fast food joint's breakfast sandwich)
1 English muffin
Ketchup
Mayonnaise

Pour a spoonful of vegetable oil into the frying pan and get it nice and hot – either over the direct heat on the grill, or over a high heat on the hob. Fry off your sausage and potato flying saucers from the planet 'I'm-gonna-beat-this-damn-hangover-atron'.

If you're outdoors, you can also put the sausage direct on the grill. Or use a plancha for everything.

Turn the sausage a couple of times until it's got a lovely char on the surface and is cooked through – about 6–8 minutes in total. The potatoes need to be left alone until they achieve a lovely golden-brown crust on the bottom – about 3 or 4 minutes. Once you have that, you can flip and rock the other side till it's good to go.

Lay things out on paper towels as they are cooked. Break the eggs into the pan or plancha and fry to your liking. Add a slice of cheese on top of each egg, just before they are done. Toast the muffin and get ready to build!

Place the fried potato flying saucer on your base, with the sausage and cheesy eggs on top. Splash some ketchup and mayo onto the top half of the muffin and finish her off.

To make this super authentic, wrap it in wax paper and let it stand for 5 minutes, so that all those flavours become one glorious beautiful thing like those breakfast burgers you eye up in McDonald's (other fast food joints are available).

# BLACK PUDDING BURGER

Black pudding is a superfood – it's official! But it was also born in the birthplace of heavy metal: Birmingham, England! It's a classic of British breakfasts and tastes amazeballs. I like adding a slice of fried black pudding to loads of my burgers but this is the ultimate incarnation of black pudding in a breakfast burger.

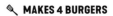

**MAKES 4 BURGERS**

**OUTDOORS** Half & half technique, with a frying pan

**INDOORS** Frying pan on the hob (stovetop)

200g (7oz) black pudding
200g (7oz) sausage meat
1 tbsp wholegrain mustard
4 large eggs
Knob of butter
4 crusty white buns or cheese-topped rolls
1 avocado, sliced
1 red onion, thinly sliced
Brown sauce or ketchup (optional)
Black pepper

First, you need to prepare your patties. Crumble up the black pudding in a bowl, then add the sausage meat and wholegrain mustard. Mix well, then break into four equal balls. Flatten them down into that perfect breakfast patty.

In another bowl, crack open your eggs and lightly whisk.

Get your grill rocking to a medium–hot heat. Get your frying pan on top and hot (or put it over a medium heat on the hob). Fry your patties, until you have a lovely crust and they're cooked through – about 6 or 8 minutes per side. There will be loads of fat rendering off the patties, which can be removed with a spoon. Too much liquid in the pan will prevent your burgers from getting a good colour on the outside. Take the patties out of the pan and lay them out on paper towels to soak up any leftover grease.

Now for the eggs. Chuck the knob of butter into your frying pan (if you're cooking indoors, give it a quick wipe first). Once it's melted, pour in your eggs and stir lightly until scrambled. Season with pepper – you don't need to use salt on this as there is plenty in the sausage meat and black pudding. Set the eggs aside and get your buns toasted.

Now it's time to assemble.

Place the burger on the bottom bun, then stack up the scrambled eggs, avocado slices and red onion, and finish with the top bun. If you want to rock a condiment in this tasty package, go for brown sauce or ketchup. Enjoy!

# NOAH'S CHEESEBURGER OMELETTE

That's right, you aren't blind. You read the title correctly – we're talking about a cheeseburger and an omelette. My son, Noah, asked me to make this for him when he was 10 years old. So, I stepped into Cluckingham Palace (our chicken hutch), grabbed me some fresh eggs, and made the boy this weirdly delicious edible delight. Instead of bread, the bun is made from an omelette pita type thing to envelop the cheeseburger patties. You don't wanna get this thing wrong – you'll have egg on your face. But if you follow these instructions eggsactly, then you'll eggspect eggscellent results. Sorry, I let T-Bone go for it with his eggsemplary puns.

---

🔪 **MAKES 1 OMELETTE; ENOUGH FOR 2 (IF YOU LIKE SHARING)**

🍖 **OUTDOORS** Half & half technique, with a frying pan

🍳 **INDOORS** Frying pan and griddle pan on the hob (stovetop)

---

3 eggs
Light olive oil or butter, for frying
½ green (bell) pepper, deseeded and sliced
½ red (bell) pepper, deseeded and sliced
½ yellow (bell) pepper, deseeded and sliced
1 red chilli pepper, deseeded and sliced
1 small red onion, sliced
4 mushrooms, sliced
200g (7oz) beef mince (ground beef)
2 slices of cheese
Sea salt and black pepper

Get your grill rocking! Then crack your eggs into a mixing bowl and whisk well. Our mate Ian Mackie (ex-chef, now sound system builder – he did our truck!) whisks two eggs nice and smooth, then cracks in the third egg and lightly folds it in to develop different textures and a lovely soft bit of egg. It's a super-righteous hack when you get it right.

Set a medium frying pan over a medium heat on the hob (or over the direct heat on the grill) with a glug of olive oil or a knob of butter and fry off all the veg until nice and soft and golden in colour.

Divide the beef mince into two balls and flatten them into patties.

Get your grill nice and hot, or set your griddle pan over a high heat on the hob. Season your patties with salt and pepper, then get cooking. If you're cooking outdoors, the meat might stick to the grill – don't worry, relax, the grill will release the meat when it's ready.

Cook for 1–2 minutes, then flip, and repeat the process until they are almost done. These burgers are best served medium. When they're almost cooked – after about 5 minutes – add the cheese slices on top of each burger and leave to melt. Use a temperature probe to make sure the burger is perfectly cooked – check the internal meat

temperatures on page 16 – then remove your burgers and keep warm while you make your omelette bun.

Heat a knob of butter in a frying pan set over a low to medium heat on the hob (or over direct heat). When it is melted, swirl the butter around the pan, then pour in the beaten eggs. Use a fork or spatula to bring it together, as this helps to make it fluffier. Play with the eggs until they

cook through. When you've got your omelette, place the cheeseburgers and cooked veg on it in the pan, then fold over. Boomtown!

Please share a photo of this so I can show it to Noah. He'll be pumped. He'll pretend he's not eggcited as he's a teenager...

Cut in half with your largest sword and then serve.

# YOU GOTTA
# BE KIDDING
# ME BURGERS!

# FISH & CHIPS BURGER

Back in 2003, I used to host a radio show called the Rock Copter, for Total Rock. The station was above a pub in south London. Across the road was *the* best fish and chips restaurant in London, run by these twin brothers. They spent their lives buying rundown fish and chip joints, rebuilding them, turning them around and flipping them for a nice profit so that they could go off travelling. When the money ran out, they would return to London and find another chippy.

These dudes taught me how to make the perfect fish and chips – it's all about the temperature of the oil. If it's not hot enough, you'll just boil the food and it won't crisp up properly. No one wants soggy chips (apart from my 11-year-old son. Weird kid). Sometimes I wouldn't finish the meal and would get a doggy bag for the next day – and that's when this burger was born. Let's do this!

---

🔪 **MAKES 4 BURGERS**

🍖 **OUTDOORS** Not recommended for frying

🍱 **INDOORS** Oven, plus saucepan on the hob (stovetop), plus deep-fat fryer or deep saucepan

---

3 or 4 baking potatoes (you'll only need 2 for the burgers but make extra to nibble on the side)
Vegetable oil, for deep-fat frying (at least 2 litres/3½ pints)
4 portions of white fish fillet (cod/ haddock/coley/plaice all work well but my fave is haddock – make each portion a bit bigger than your bun)
Malt vinegar
4 soft white buns
Sea salt and black pepper

First, let's get those chips rocking. The best chips come from baked potatoes. It's pretty much like doing a twice-cooked chip! Make them the day before, as the potatoes need to cool completely before deep-frying.

Preheat the oven to 180°C (350°F/gas mark 4). Bake your potatoes for 45–60 minutes. Pull them out and let them cool. When you're ready to fry, cut the potatoes into chip-like wedges.

Batter batter, hey BATTER! Batter up! Whisk the flour, beer and a pinch of salt and pepper in a large bowl until smooth. Or as smooth as you can – don't worry if there are a couple of lumps.

Empty your tin of peas into a small saucepan. Add the butter and stir over a low heat on the hob (or indirect heat on the outdoor grill) for 10 minutes until mushy. Season with salt and pepper.

Mix all your tartare sauce ingredients together in a bowl and set aside, ready for the build.

Now for the interesting part! Pour the oil into a large deep saucepan (or you can use a deep-fat fryer) – it needs to be about half-filled.

*Ingredients and recipe continue...*

## BATTER

200g (7oz/1⅔ cup) self-raising (self-rising) flour, plus extra for dusting
300ml (10½fl oz/1¼ cups) beer

## MUSHY PEAS

1 × 300g (10oz) can marrowfat peas
30g (1oz/2 tbsp) butter

## TARTARE SAUCE

100g (3½oz/scant ½ cup) mayonnaise
1 gherkin (pickle), finely chopped
1 tbsp capers, finely chopped
½ tsp English mustard
1 tbsp cider vinegar
1 tbsp chopped flat-leaf parsley

*Recipe continued from page 38.*

Set it over a high heat and get that oil hot. Once the temperature reaches 180°C (350°F), you are good to fry.

Chuck some flour on a plate or chopping board and press your fish in it until it is lightly coated with flour. Now dip the fish into the batter so that it's completely covered. Pull it out and let the excess batter drip off, then carefully slip the battered fish into the hot oil.

Leave to cook for 6–7 minutes until golden brown. Remove the fish onto a paper towel with a slotted spoon, and repeat. While your fish is resting, season with malt vinegar, salt and pepper.

When your fish is done, it's time to batch-fry your chips. Make sure the temperature is still at 180°C (350°F), then carefully lower a handful of chips into the oil. Cook for 1–2 minutes until golden brown and crispy. Remove and drain alongside the fish. Season with salt.

When everything is cooked, it's time to build this next-level burger.

Slather the mushy peas on the bottom bun, top with a handful of chips, then 'plaice' the fish on top. (Get it?! Plaice! Like the fish. It's the 'sole' reason to include this recipe. Oh, for 'cod's' sake. Sorry.) Spoon the tartare sauce onto the fish, then finish with the other half of the bun.

Wow! Yeah, you just did that! You made an almighty fish and chips burger. Well done, you wonderful member of Earth! Now get eating. And save some for us!

# SUNDAY ROAST CHICKEN BURGER

Everyone loves a Sunday roast, especially when it comes with all the fixings. How about a Sunday roast that you can hold in the palm of your hand? With all the fixings? Well, I made it, and it was way beyond my expectations. And then I smothered it in gravy, taking it to the upper atmosphere of deliciousness and messiness.

The easiest way to make this burger is to use the leftovers from your Sunday roast. But, if you don't have that luxury, then here's the complete method for making the ultimate Sunday lunch burger.

> 🍴 **MAKES 6 BURGERS**
>
> 🍖 **OUTDOORS** Kettle-style grill with lid (or hot smoker), half & half technique
>
> 🗓 **INDOORS** Oven and hob (stovetop)
>
> You'll need two roasting tins (pans) and a muffin tray with at least six holes

6 brioche buns,
½ green cabbage, sliced

## ROAST CHICKEN

1 medium chicken
Olive oil
Sprig of fresh rosemary, chopped
1 onion, peeled and quartered
1 carrot, chopped
1 whole garlic bulb, halved
Sea salt and black pepper

## ROAST VEG

3 large potatoes, quartered
100g (3½oz/scant ½ cup) beef
   dripping
3 carrots, quartered
3 parsnips, quartered

## YORKSHIRE PUDDING

100g (3½oz/generous ¾ cup) plain
   (all-purpose) flour
100ml (3½fl oz/scant ½ cup)
   beaten eggs (about 2–3 eggs)
100ml (3½fl oz/scant ½ cup) milk
100g (3½oz/scant ½ cup) beef
   dripping

## GRAVY

500ml (17fl oz/generous 2 cups)
   chicken stock
2 tbsp plain (all-purpose) flour

## BREAD SAUCE

500ml (17fl oz/generous 2 cups)
   full-fat (whole) milk
10 cloves
2 bay leaves
1 tsp black peppercorns
1 tbsp butter

Get your outdoor grill rocking or preheat your oven to 180°C (350°F/gas mark 4).

Oil the chicken, and sprinkle over the rosemary, salt and pepper. Place the chicken in a roasting tin, along with the onion, carrot and garlic, and stick it in the oven. If you're cooking outdoors, put the tin straight onto the grill over the indirect heat and close the cooker lid. Leave it to cook for about an hour, until cooked through to a core temperature of 72°C (162°F).

While the chicken is cooking, you need to prepare your roast potatoes. Boil the spuds for about 15 minutes until nearly cooked through. Drain into a colander and leave to cool and dry.

Whisk together the flour, eggs and milk for the Yorkshire pudding, season and set aside.

When the chicken is ready, leave it to rest on a plate in a warm place for at least 30 minutes (keeping the veg in the tin). This is the most important part of cooking a chicken (apart from the heat part). Turn the oven up to 220°C (425°F/ gas mark 7) or whack some more fuel into your grill and get it hot.

Put the beef dripping (for the roast veg) in another roasting tin and heat in the oven or on the outdoor grill until smoking hot. Add the par-cooked spuds to the hot dripping in their tin, along with the carrots and parsnips. Roast in the oven or on the grill with the cooker lid closed for about 30–40 minutes until crispy, turning every so often. Damn these things are good... drain on paper towels when done.

While the potatoes and veg are roasting, divide the beef dripping for the Yorkshire pudding into six holes of a muffin tray, and heat that in the oven until smoking hot as well. Then, pour the batter mix into the dripping and slam back in the oven. Let your puddings of savoury beauty puff up but be careful not to take them out of the oven too early as you want them nice and golden (about 20–25 minutes).

Meanwhile, make the gravy. Take your veg left over from cooking the chicken and place over a medium heat – either on the hob or over direct heat. Whisk the flour into the fat making sure you don't have any lumps, then pour in the chicken stock. Simmer for 20 minutes, stirring frequently, until thick brown. Strain through a sieve into a jug (discarding the veg) and keep warm.

While the gravy is simmering, get started on your bread sauce. Roughly chop up the bread bun bottoms – 'What am I gonna serve all this food on, you crazy lunatic?' – well, you will find out next episode (in about two paragraphs' time). Add these to a small pan with the rest of the bread sauce ingredients. Simmer over a gentle heat (hob or indirect heat on the grill) for about 5 minutes, stirring all the time, until thick and creamy. Season with a little salt.

Finally, boil the cabbage in salted water (hob or direct heat on the grill) for 5 minutes. Drain and set aside. Season with salt and pepper.

Now, you are almost there to turn this titan of Sunday afternoons into the most handy hand snack ever! Carve your chicken into six juicy pieces (two breasts, two drumsticks, two thighs). Cut each breast into two and remove the bones from the drumsticks and thighs (the thighs make probably the best two burgers – save them for you and your best buddy).

Lay out your Yorkshire puddings and fill each one with a chunk of roasted potato, carrot and parsnip. Make sure you munch on the extras as you go! Follow with a large pinch of cabbage and some roast chicken. If you don't think it can take any more... it will. Don't give up!

Spoon bread sauce all over the chicken, add the bun tops and you're almost done... Just before you hit your buddies with this most Sunday of burgers, pour a gallon of gravy all over. If you don't want it too messy, pour it on under the lid so you get a little pool in your Yorkshire base. Radelicious!

# MOMMA'S GRAVY BOAT BURGER

When my momma first served this tasty southern dish, I couldn't believe it. Pulling a burger out of a big ol' vat of gravy! Moist, savoury, super-juicy and dripping with tasty gravy… why isn't this a normal thing for every family in America? This should be celebrated worldwide. Momma would serve it on a bed of mash and smother the whole lot with more gravy. My version is more like an open-faced burger sandwich. Let's rock! I wanna rock! I wanna grab my favourite tongs and dip them into that retro 1975 gravy bowl and pull out that delicious gravy-soaked burger right now!

🍴 **SERVES 5**

🍗 **OUTDOORS** Half & half technique, with frying pan or plancha; or direct on the grill

🍳 **INDOORS** Oven, plus saucepan and griddle or frying pan on the hob (stovetop)

You'll also need a roasting tin (pan)

## QUICK GRAVY

(A quicker gravy would involve gravy granules and that's cool – we've all done it – but this one will taste a lot better!)

50g (1¾oz) butter
2 red onions, peeled and quartered
2 carrots, chopped
1 whole garlic bulb, halved
2 celery sticks, chopped
2 bacon rashers (slices), chopped
500ml (17fl oz/generous 2 cups) beef stock
1–3 tbsp plain (all-purpose) flour (depending on how thick ya like your gravy)

Get your outdoor grill rocking or preheat your oven to 180°C (350°F/gas mark 4).

Gravy time! Throw the butter, veg and bacon into a roasting tin and cook in the oven or over direct heat on the grill for 25–30 minutes, until it's all nice and golden.

When the veg is ready, place the roasting tin on a medium heat – either on the hob or the grill, and whisk in the flour until it soaks up the lovely fat, then add in the beef stock and let it come up to a boil. Simmer for 20 minutes, stirring frequently, until you have one hell of a beefy-looking gravy.

Meanwhile, get a large saucepan of water boiling – either on the hob or over the direct heat. Carefully lower in your spuds and cook for 12–18 minutes, until tender.

Drain all the excess water, then add the milk, butter, pepper and salt. Mash the potatoes until creamy and awesomey (new word alert). Then cover and set aside.

When the gravy is ready, strain through a sieve into a large bowl (with a lid to keep it all nice and hot), discarding all the veg. Keep it warm somewhere, while you get those burgers rocking.

*Ingredients and recipe continues…*

## MASHED POTATOES

8 large potatoes, peeled and
  quartered
200ml (7fl oz/generous
  ¾ cup) milk
200g (7oz) butter
1 tsp white pepper
1 tsp salt

## BURGERS

1kg (2lb 4oz) beef mince
  (ground beef)
5 burger buns
Sea salt and black pepper

*Recipe continued from page 46.*

If you're cooking indoors, get your griddle pan nice and hot on the hob. Outdoors, you can cook direct on the grill or set your plancha or frying pan over the direct heat.

Break the mince into 10 balls and flatten into patties. Season with salt and pepper and grill the burgers for about 5–10 minutes, flipping occasionally to create a lovely crust. Place the burgers on paper towels to drain off the excess fat, then put them in the gravy bowl and cover.

Set that dining table up with the burger/gravy bowl as the centrepiece, surrounded by a vat of creamy mash and plate of buns. You'll probably want to have some lovely veg sides to go along with your epic meal – I like corn and green beans, but this is your feast and I am here to help you with the main event.

Serving time! Open up the burger buns and slam down some mash onto each bun. Use your tongs to pull out two beef patties and place them on the bed of mash. Grab a ladle and cover your mountain of awesomeness with that delicious gravy. Man, this is reminding me of my childhood. I want this dish now... why does my mom gotta live so far away?! In the immortal words of Ozzy Osbourne, 'Momma, I'm coming home for your gravy boat burger and mash open-faced sandwich.'

# STEAK TARTARE BURGER

I came up with this recipe of radness when thinking of some kind of ridiculously tender cut of beef for a burger. That cut had to be a fillet steak (filet mignon for our North American brethren). I then thought cooking it would actually be a crime. Maybe some kind of cool crime like racketeering and taking money from the rich to give to the poor, a Robin Hood kinda crime – I hate you Sheriff of Nottingham! Sorry, back to this burger of insanity...

---

🔪 **MAKES 2 BURGERS**

🍖 **OUTDOORS** Half & half technique, with a frying pan or plancha

🍳 **INDOORS** Frying pan on the hob (stovetop)

---

300–350g (10½–12oz) fillet steak
1 medium gherkin (pickle), finely chopped
1 tbsp capers, very finely chopped
1 small shallot, very very finely chopped
Dash of Tabasco sauce
2 brioche buns (go decadent!)
2 free range egg yolks, cracked into separate cups
Sea salt and black pepper

You need to move quickly here, folks.

Keep the fillet in the fridge until you are ready to prepare. Normally, you'd want those steaks out of the fridge at least an hour before cooking but not this time. When you are ready to go, place the steak on a chopping board and slice off a thin layer all the way around the outside. You can only really eat raw the beef that hasn't touched the air.

If you're cooking outdoors, get your grill nice and hot and place your plancha or frying pan over the direct heat. Indoors, get your frying pan nice and hot on a high heat.

Finely dice the fillet and mix with the chopped gherkin, capers and shallot. Add a dash of Tabasco and season with salt and pepper.

Toast your buns. Brioche will burn quick so they don't need much time in the pan.

Form two patties with the beef mix. They might need a bit of cajoling with your hands. When ready, have a fish slice in hand – the next bit is quick. Gently place the patties onto the hot surface and sear super quickly – 30 seconds max! Once you have a light browning, carefully turn over and give them another 20–30 seconds.

Place the burgers straight onto the toasted bun bottoms. Make a dimple with a spoon in the middle of each burger and slide on an egg yolk. Crown the burger with the brioche bun top, wait to be knighted by Sir Beefalot, then feast upon this jewel of meaty tenderness. So hot! But really kinda lukewarm.

# CHAR SIU BURGER

**Who doesn't like munching on some steamy Chinese BBQ pork? This is based on the classic Char Siu Bao but using a normal bun so anyone can rock this recipe.**

---

🥄 **MAKES 4 BURGERS**

🍖 **OUTDOORS** Half & half technique

📱 **INDOORS** Hob (stovetop)

You'll also need a casserole pot with a lid, a frying pan and a steamer

---

1.2kg (1lb 10oz) boneless pork belly, butterflied, rolled and tied
1 bunch of spring onions (scallions), sliced
1 red chilli, finely sliced
1 tbsp toasted sesame seeds
4 plain white buns

### GLAZE FOR PORK
1 litre (35fl oz/4¼ cups) water
250ml (9fl oz/generous 1 cup) orange juice
150ml (5fl oz/⅔ cup) light soy sauce
150ml (5fl oz/⅔ cup) rice wine
4 tbsp oyster sauce
½ tsp sesame oil
2.5cm (1-inch) piece of ginger, peeled and sliced
5 garlic cloves, sliced
2 cinnamon sticks
2 star anise
1 red chilli, sliced

### PICKLED CUCUMBER
100ml (3½fl oz/scant ½ cup) rice vinegar
100g (3½oz) caster (superfine) sugar
1 tbsp black peppercorns
½ cucumber, sliced

If you're cooking outdoors, get your grill rocking.

Add all the glaze ingredients to a casserole pot and place it either over a medium heat on the hob or over the direct heat on the grill.

Say a few kind words to your pork belly, then add it to the pot, bring to the boil, put on the lid and leave to simmer slowly for 2 hours until tender.

While the pork is cooking, pickle your cucumber. This little delight will cut through that rich pork belly. In a small saucepan over a low heat, heat the vinegar and sugar together with the peppercorns, until the sugar has dissolved. Let it cool, then pour over the sliced cucumber. Leave for 30 minutes until the cucumber is tangy.

When the pork is cooked, remove it from the casserole pot, wrap it in cling film (plastic wrap) and cool for 30 minutes. Pour the remaining sweet-swelling liquid from the pot into a large frying pan and set over a medium heat on the hob (or over direct heat on the grill) and reduce until it is thick. This will take at least 30 minutes. Once the glaze is thick and shiny, leave to cool.

Slice the cooled pork into four thick burgers and add to the cooled glaze pan. Put the pan back on a medium heat (or the grill), and spoon the glaze over the pork slices.

Once they are sticky and have a nice colour on them, get your steamer ready – put it on the heat source (hob or grill) and place a square of baking (parchment) paper in it.

Layer up the glazed pork belly, spring onions, chilli slices, sesame seeds and pickled cucumber in the bun. Place on the paper in the steamer and steam for 5 minutes until hot and soft. Serve with any extra glaze as a dipping sauce.

# QUAD BURGER

I went on a taco tour of California for my YouTube channel. My last day was in LA, and I got to hang with Chris Guanlao, drummer in Silversun Pickups – I love that band! I asked him what I should order at In-N-Out Burger as I'd never been there before. Chris said, '4X4'. So that's what I got. And this is my interpretation of that In-N-Out off-menu favourite.

---

🍴 **FEEDS YOU!**

🍖 **OUTDOORS** Half & half technique

📟 **INDOORS** Frying pan or griddle pan on the hob (stovetop)

You'll need a cloche or large metal bowl to use as a lid

---

230–280g (8–10oz) beef mince (ground beef), min. 20% fat content
1 burger bun (the smaller in diameter the better)
3 pickle slices
4 slices of burger cheese
Ketchup
American yellow mustard

**QUAD SEASONING LIGHTNING RUB OF DOOM**
1 tbsp sea salt
1 tbsp white pepper
1 tsp garlic granules
1 tsp onion granules

---

Break the mince into four balls. Gently flatten each ball, so that the patty is slightly bigger than the bun, unless you got some crazy-ass goliath bun. This might sound insane but the thinner those patties are, the more Maillard reaction your eager taste buds get to feast on. Also, you'll get some shrinkage as the fats render while it cooks. And remember, you do have to get your laughing gear around four of these suckers.

Make the Quad Seasoning Lightning Rub of Doom by mixing together all the ingredients, then sprinkle onto the beef patties. Get your cooking surface nice and hot – either a rocking fire on your grill, or frying or griddle pan set over a high heat on your hob – and throw down those patties like Thor unleashing the hammer (but then Korg starts telling stories of Doug, and all I want is Korg the Movie).

Get a good sear on one side. You want it sizzling. Nice and hot! And while it's doing its thing, get your bun toasted. Once you have a nice crust on the burgers – a matter of 3 or 4 minutes on each side – turn over and lace each one with a cheese slice. Cover with a cloche or big old metal bowl to speed up the melt on the cheese. Cook for another 3 or 4 minutes and get everything ready for a quick build.

The bottom bun is bare. Upon it, place each cheeseburger, one on top of the other. This is more than most buns can handle. Add the pickle slices. Squirt the lid with ketchup and mustard and top that burger off. Lord have mercy! This is a heavenly titan of titanic meaty proportions!

# BEER BOTTLE BURGER

This has got to be one of the most fun burgers to put together. If you ever wanted to play with your food before getting stuck in, then this is the recipe for you, inspired by the BBQ Pit Boys. They have the number one BBQ channel on YouTube and always put a smile on my face. They make this recipe with a beer can but I like using a bottle as I find the mince doesn't stick to the glass as easily. This is a big burger, so bring your appetite and some patience. It takes a bit of time to achieve this greatness.

---

🔧 **MAKES 2 BIG BURGERS**

🍴 **OUTDOORS** Kettle-style grill with a lid, half & half technique, with a plancha or frying pan

🍳 **INDOORS** Frying pan on the hob (stovetop), then oven

---

Light olive oil or vegetable oil, for frying
6 mushrooms, chopped
1 onion, chopped
½ green (bell) pepper, sliced
½ red (bell) pepper, sliced
½ yellow (bell) pepper, sliced
300–400g (10½–14oz) beef mince (ground beef) – you can go as big as you like for this!
1 × 330ml (11fl oz) bottle of beer
12 streaky bacon rashers (slices), stretched for maximum coverage
150g (5½oz) cheddar cheese, grated (shredded)
2 slices of burger cheese
2 large burger buns
Ketchup
American yellow mustard
Sea salt and black pepper

First, get your grill rocking or preheat your oven to 180°C (350°F/gas mark 4).

This baby requires a bit of prep as you'll want to have all your ingredients ready to go into the meat bowl you are about to create. So, without further ado, let's brown off the veg.

Set a large frying pan over a medium heat on the hob or direct heat on the grill and add a glug of oil in. When the oil is hot, throw in your veg. Keep the mushrooms separate from the onions and peppers, as it will help to give the veggies that golden colour. Cook for about 5 minutes until they are softened, season, then set aside and get ready to play at pottery with your beef.

Divide the mince into two equal piles, then form these into big old balls on a chopping board or work surface. Place your bottle of beer into one of the balls and push down, creating a meat bowl. You'll want to have a decent base, so don't push the bottle through the meat – keep 1–2cm (½–1 inch) of beef under the bottle. Now ease the meat up the sides of the beer bottle – pretend you are Patrick Swayze in Ghost and you are helping Demi Moore with her pottery. Keep shaping the beef mince around the bottle until it's uniform and sits about 8–10cm (3–4 inches) high. Now, carefully wrap the stretched bacon around the beef mince, making sure that none of the meat is exposed.

*Recipe continues...*

*Recipe continued from page 56.*

Here's the tricky bit – getting that bottle out of the burger. Gently twist the bottle and slowly pull it out. You'll probably have to twist and pull a couple of times until the meat gives in and lets you have your beer back. Give it a wash and enjoy that beer.

Now let's fill that meat bowl with all that lovely grilled veg. Using tongs, put one layer of veg into the bowl to come about halfway. Then sprinkle some grated cheese on top, then add more grilled veg onto that layer until it reaches the top. Grab some more cheese and completely cover the veg and the top of the beef bowl. Cover with a slice of burger cheese on top to make it extra awesome.

The next step can be precarious so go carefully. Ease a spatula under the burger bowl and gently place it on the indirect side of your grill, and pop the lid of the grill on.

If you're indoors, then place the burger on a baking sheet and bake in the oven for 20–25 minutes. You want to cook the burger until the bacon has a lovely colour and the beef mince has hit an internal temperature of at least 68°C (154°F). If you're cooking outdoors and you want to get a good char, feel free to move the burger over some direct heat for a bit. Just be careful not to make a hole in the bottom of the burger.

Toast your buns, squirt ketchup and mustard over them and then bookend that edible beer bottle burger bowl with your buns.

Make sure you take some pictures of this and upload 'em to social media. You are bound to get a load of likes for this creation.

# LAMB SHAWARMA BURGER

I've travelled the seven seas to bring you the world's tastiest burger. Yes, you are welcome, but really it was my pleasure. I got to skate, snowboard, surf all over the place and I met some incredible people along the way. I sampled the globe's delights and came away with this bad boy! Wooooooohoooooooo... I want to go back on the road!

---

✎ **MAKES 4 BURGERS**

🍖 **OUTDOORS** Kettle-style grill with lid, half & half technique

🔲 **INDOORS** Not recommended for the lamb – this works best on the grill to get a good char

---

½ boned-out butterflied lamb shoulder, around 1–1.5kg (2lb 4oz–3lb)
8 cherry tomatoes
1 tbsp olive oil
1 tbsp balsamic vinegar
Sprig of thyme, leaves picked
4 ciabatta buns or flatbreads
8 baby gem lettuce leaves
1 small red onion, thinly sliced
Pickled jalapeños or chillies
100ml (3½fl oz/scant ½ cup) natural (plain) yogurt
Sea salt

**SPICE MIX**

2 tsp salt
1 tsp garlic granules
½ tsp ground turmeric
1 tsp ground cumin
1 tsp ground coriander
1 tsp paprika
½ tsp cayenne
½ tsp ground cinnamon

This is a big one, so you need to get started early so you can blow away your friends and family with its deliciousness.

Trim off any gristle and flatten out the butterflied shoulder with a rolling pin. Using a sharp knife, cut the lamb into 10cm-wide (4-inch) pieces.

Stir all the ingredients for the spice mix together in a bowl, then rub it all over the lamb. Make sure the meat is evenly covered with the spice mix.

Good luck with this next bit – you will need a steady hand. Neatly stack the lamb pieces on a chopping board. Holding the pile of lamb secure with the finger and thumb of one hand: use a long and skinny sharp knife to pierce through the middle of all the lamb pieces, vertically from top to bottom.

Keeping the knife in place, take a long metal spoon and slide the handle down the flat side of the knife, so you can replace the knife with the spoon. Nice work! How does that feel? You are making a proper lamb shawarma. Pick up the end of the spoon and make sure the lamb is secure.

Place the lamb over direct heat on the grill. Once you get a good char on the meat, turn it, until the whole of the outside is cooked. Then move the lamb to the indirect side of the grill, and put the lid on to make sure the middle is properly cooked through or at least blushing – lamb is best served medium, this could take 30–45 minutes.

*Recipe continues...*

*Recipe continued from page 60.*

When it's cooked, the lamb needs to rest for about 10 minutes, which gives you plenty of time to roast your cherry tomatoes. Stick them in a small roasting tin (pan), drizzle with the olive oil and balsamic vinegar, then sprinkle with thyme leaves and salt. Put the tin on the grill, return the lid and roast until tender, about 15 minutes. If you're doing this indoors, make sure you preheat your oven to 200°C (400°F/gas mark 6) first.

Toast your buns and get ready for the build, as this is gonna be epic.

When the meat is ready, holding the spoon upright, carve downwards to slice the meat off it.

Bottom bun first, then 2 lettuce leaves per bun. Place a good portion of lamb chunks on the lettuce. Follow that with the red onions and pickled jalapeños. Drizzle some yogurt onto all this goodness, and top with the tomatoes and bun.

Right? Right! Do it, serve 'em up and enjoy. T-Bone Chops and I are stoked for ya. We really are, as this is a beast of a recipe.

# THE KING BURGER

I love Johnny Cash, Stevie Wonder, Frank Sinatra, Elton John, Madonna, Barry Manilow, Andy Williams, John Farnham, Iggy Pop, Dolly Parton and Jimi Hendrix. But the TRUE King of Music is Elvis Presley. I wanted to create a burger that he would be proud of. There's enough protein in this to feed a human for a good couple of months. This burger is so massive and indulgent, it should only be attempted once a decade... nah, make that once every other decade. It's been called the 'Ultimeatum', 'Meatageddon', 'The Massive', 'The Heart Attack Special', 'The Time Machine' and 'Captain Beef-lungs'. But its true name is The King Burger in honour of Elvis and his stage outfits (Google 'Elvis Presley Suspicious Minds Live in Las Vegas' – other search engines are available). When I first made this, I was a bit dubious about the peanut butter and jam. But holy crap! It works really really well! Take it from me, this burger is royally delicious!

🥄 **FEEDS 1 KING**

🍖 **OUTDOORS** Half & half technique, with a plancha (optional, but helps with the bacon); not recommended for the deep-fried onion rings and banana

🍳 **INDOORS** Frying pan or griddle pan on the hob (stovetop)

You'll also need a deep-fat fryer or deep saucepan, and a cloche or large metal bowl to use as a lid

250g (9oz) beef mince (ground beef)

7 streaky bacon rashers (slices)

Vegetable oil, for deep-fat frying (at least 2 litres/3½ pints)

Sea salt and black pepper

## DEEP-FRIED ONION RINGS & BANANA

100g (3½oz/¾ cup) self-raising (self-rising) flour

150ml (5fl oz/⅔ cup) beer

Pinch of salt

1 tbsp demerara sugar

1 banana, sliced lengthways and halved into 4

1 white onion, sliced into thick rings

## TO SERVE – TOPPINGS ETC

Dollop of peanut butter (chunky and crunchy is good, but smooth works killer too)

Dollop of jam (try the classic grape flavour – grape jelly, as it's known in the USA)

2 slices of mature cheddar cheese (Red Leicester/Monterey Jack also rock)

2 slices of burger cheese

1 big old burger bun

2 dollops of mayonnaise

1 gherkin, sliced lengthways

There is a lot to do here, so you'll need to manage your timings on this one. Get everything prepped and all your toppings laid out. Combine the peanut butter and jam/jelly in a little bowl.

Make the batter for the deep-fried onion rings and banana by combining the flour, beer and salt in a mixing bowl and whisking until smooth. Put the sugar in a shallow bowl and coat your banana bits in it.

This is a big burger so it's best to get the bacon and burger cooked first, and then you can make the deep-fried onion rings and banana pieces while the burger is resting. Ooooh, just typing that last sentence made my heart stop for a second. Phew, there it goes again.

Get your grill nice and hot (and plancha, if using), or set your frying pan or griddle pan over a medium to high heat on the hob.

Shape up the beef mince into one big ol' patty. Good luck keeping it together! This is a lot of meat to sculpt, so take your time and shape a patty worthy of Elvis and your appetite. If the size of the patty is a bit frightening, then good! It should be.

Chuck your bacon into the frying pan or plancha and cook it off until crispy. Season the patty with salt and pepper and place it over the direct heat or into the pan. It's a huge beast, so you'll need to move it around to get the middle cooked without burning the outside; you want a slow crust to build up, as it's a thick piece of meat to cook. If you're cooking outdoors, the meat might stick to the grill – don't worry, relax, the grill will release the meat when it's ready.

Cook for a couple of minutes, until you have a nice sear on the bottom, then flip the burger and work the other side until there's a crust forming on the bottom again. Once you have a good crust on both sides of the patty, move it over indirect heat, so that the middle of the patty can increase in temperature. Move that patty between direct heat and indirect heat until it is almost done

(about 10 minutes in total). This burger is best medium rare.

Layer the cheese slices on top of the patty and cover with a cloche or big old metal bowl to speed up the melt on the cheese (it'll take max 30 seconds this way). Use a temperature probe and check the internal meat temperatures on page 16 – then remove your burgers and keep warm while you get deep-frying.

Pour the oil into a large, deep saucepan (or you can use a deep-fat fryer), set it over a high heat and get that oil hot. Once the temperature reaches 180°C (350°F), you are good to fry.

Dip your banana pieces and onion rings into the batter, then fry them until golden (about 3 or 4 minutes).

Toast your bun and slather each half in an obscene amount of mayo.

Begin the stack with the mayo-y bun, the king patty, followed by dollops of peanut butter and jelly mixture, all the bacon, some deep-fried banana, gherkin, the mayo-y top bun and then a sword to hold it together. Or a large knife. Throw some onion rings on top and there you have it. The King Burger!

*P.S. After writing the recipe, T-Bone and I think it's best that you should never attempt this burger. Please, we beg of you – don't ever make this burger! But if you do, please share photos so we can put them up on the DJ BBQ IG!*

# BANGING
# BURGERS

# DJ BBQ BURGER

This is the most DJ BBQy burger that DJ BBQ has ever cooked on a BBQ. Although, actually BBQ is the food and not the grill, but people still call the grill the BBQ – just a heads up people. If you are looking to make the perfect burger, then look no further. This, my friends, is it! It's a blend of different cuts of beef, so if you can't source them from a butcher just go for a decent fatty beef mince (ground beef) – minimum 20% fat! Oh boy oh boy oh boy... I'm so excited for your mouth. Uh huh! Cos it's gonna be munching on this perfect thang! This is the best-tasting beef burger ever conceived, created, invented and feasted upon. Good luck, captain!

---

🔪 **MAKES 4 BURGERS**

🍴 **OUTDOORS** Half & half technique, with frying pan

📅 **INDOORS** Oven, plus frying pan and griddle pan on the hob (stovetop)

You'll also need a cloche or large metal bowl to use as a lid

---

## BEEF PATTIES

800g (1lb 12oz) beef mince (ground beef). Ask your butcher to prepare the following mix of cuts (preferably 21–28-day dry-aged beef). You can do it yourself if you prefer – follow the weights and/or percentages below and simply put it all through a coarse grain mincer (meat grinder)

240g (8½oz) chuck (30%)
160g (5½oz) short rib (20%)
120g (4¼oz) brisket (15%)
120g (4¼oz) flank (15%)
160g (5½oz) suet or bone marrow (20%)
Sea salt and black pepper

First off, let's get the garlic for the aioli roasted. Get a load of coals rocking on your grill or preheat your oven to 180°C (350°F/gas mark 4). Loosely wrap the garlic bulb in foil and chuck it in the oven or nestle it in the coals. Leave it there for an hour. Remove and let it cool.

When it has cooled, peel four of the cloves – or you can just squeeze the oozy garlic into a bowl. Smash the garlic until super smooth. Add the rest of the aioli ingredients, and blend together well until smooth and gooey.

Season with salt and stir in the lemon juice. There's your condiment – aioli. It's enough for this recipe – but you might as well use up all your oozy cloves and make loads cos it's phenomenal on everything apart from breakfast cereal. Although I've never tried that, so maybe it's great!

Now, let's get the onions going. Place a small frying pan over indirect heat on the grill, or on a low to medium heat on the hob. Pour in the olive oil, then chuck in the knob of butter. When the butter has melted, add in the sliced onions and brown sugar. Slow-cook and stir until soft and golden – it should take around 20 minutes. Once golden, stir in the Worcestershire sauce, then keep this on a super-low heat until you are ready to serve.

*Ingredients and recipe continue...*

## AIOLI (OPTIONAL, YOU CAN ALSO USE MAYONNAISE)

1 whole garlic bulb
75ml (2½fl oz/scant ⅓ cup) olive oil
Squeeze of lemon juice
1 tbsp water
Sea salt

## ONIONS

2 tbsp olive oil
Knob of butter
2 red onions, thinly sliced
1 tbsp brown sugar
1 tsp Worcestershire sauce

## TO COOK/SERVE

4 tbsp American yellow mustard
4 slices of Monterey Jack cheese
8 dry-cured streaky bacon rashers (slices)
4 demi-brioche seeded burger buns
4 lettuce leaves
1 beef tomato, sliced

*Recipe continued from page 71.*

Divide the beef mince into four meaty balls and flatten them into patties a little bit larger than the buns, as you will get shrinkage as the fats render. Season with salt and pepper.

Have your American yellow mustard ready in a bowl with a basting brush. This is an awesome hack for making killer burgers – loads of top chefs use this mustard-basting technique.

Get your grill nice and hot, or set your griddle pan over a high heat on the hob, then slap your patties on. If you're cooking outdoors, the meat might stick to the grill – don't worry, the grill will release the meat when it's ready. You want to sear the bottom of the patties and get a nice crust (around 1–2 minutes), then flip them over and brush on some of the mustard.

When the other side has developed a crust (after another 1–2 minutes), flip the burger again and brush on more mustard. Now it's all about cooking that sweet, sharp, tangy goodness into the meat until it's where you want it. Give the burger a couple of flips until the mustard is pretty much cooked into the patty.

When they're almost cooked – after about 8 minutes – add the cheese slices on top of each burger and cover with a cloche or big old metal bowl to speed up the melt on the cheese (it'll take max 30 seconds). Use a temperature probe to make sure the burgers are perfectly cooked – check the internal meat temperatures on page 16 – then remove and keep warm.

Slam your bacon onto the grill or griddle until crispy. Remove onto paper towels to drain. Now toast your buns and lay them out for the build. Spread the bottom bun with the aioli, then add the lettuce and cheesy burger. Top with the bacon, tomato, sautéed onions, and finally the lid. You'll probably need a carjack to open up your jaw for this one – I should call it the lockjaw burger! Enjoy. You deserve it, as it was a ball-ache to make.

# THE CLASSIC CHEESEBURGER

**It wouldn't be a burger book without the classic cheeseburger. This one and the Fast Burger (page 79) will probably be your two go-to burger recipes for life.**

---

🔪 **MAKES 4 BURGERS**

🍖 **OUTDOORS** Half & half technique

🍳 **INDOORS** Griddle pan on the hob (stovetop)

You'll also need a cloche or large metal bowl to use as a lid

---

600g (14oz) beef mince (ground beef) (min. 20% fat content)
4 slices of your favourite cheese
4 seeded burger buns
½ iceberg lettuce, shredded
8 dill pickle slices
1 red onion, finely sliced
4 beef tomato slices
Favourite condiments (mayo, ketchup and American yellow mustard all rock)
Sea salt and black pepper

Divide the beef mince into four balls and flatten them into patties a little bit larger than the buns, as you will get shrinkage as the fats render. Don't make your patties too neat and compact, as you want the fats to render and work around the meat while it's cooking. You want to create fjords of beefy fat flavour on the outside of the burger!

Get your grill nice and hot, or set your griddle pan over a high heat on the hob. Season your patties with salt and pepper, then get cooking. If you're cooking outdoors, the meat might stick to the grill – don't worry, the grill will release the meat when it's ready.

Cook for 1–2 minutes, then flip, and repeat the process until they are almost done. These burgers are best served medium. When they're almost cooked – after about 6 minutes – add the cheese slices on top of each burger and cover with a cloche or large metal bowl to speed up the melt on the cheese (you'll wait only 30 seconds for cheesy goodness). Use a temperature probe to make sure the burger is perfectly cooked – check the internal meat temperatures on page 16 – then remove your burgers and keep warm while you toast the buns.

Get ready for the burger build! First, bottom bun with some mayo. Next, shredded lettuce, then burger, two pickle slices, onion, tomato slice and finally the ketchup and mustard and top bun.

But it's your burger – you're gonna be eating it – so do it your way if you like. Put the lettuce on top, scrap the mayo – it's your call. And there we have it. A solid burger for your repertoire.

# FAST BURGER

This burger is fast to make and fast to eat. It could only be faster if you dragged it behind your car and hit the A303 once you get past the Stonehenge traffic. Man, I should do a Stonehenge Burger!

---

🔧 **MAKES 1 BURGER** (If your kids or friends are really hungry, then just double or triple or whatever up)

🍴 **OUTDOORS** Half & half technique, with a plancha

🍳 **INDOORS** Frying pan on the hob (stovetop)

You'll also need a cloche or large metal bowl to use as a lid

---

115g (4oz) beef mince (ground beef)
1 burger bun
1 slice of burger cheese
Favourite condiments (mayo, ketchup and American yellow mustard are all awesome!)
Sea salt and black pepper

Make a ball with your beef and roll it out to a patty 0.5cm (¼-inch) thick. Season with salt and pepper.

Get your cooking surface nice and hot – either sit your plancha over direct heat on the grill or your frying pan over a high heat on the hob.

Then place that fast patty onto the plancha or into the frying pan. This is fast – no time to waste, time's a-ticking! Chop chop. Choppy choppy!

Get a nice crust on your burger and flip to get that same crust on the other side – a matter of 2 or 3 minutes each side. These burgers are best served medium. So, when that burger is almost ready, add the cheese slice on top followed by the bun lid, then sprinkle a tablespoon of water around the patty. Quickly cover with a cloche or large lid. Get that steam working into the bread. It won't take more than 10 or 20 seconds. You are running out of time! Slam that cheesy beefy goodness onto the bottom bun.

The top bun has already made friends with the cheeseburger. Squirt your condiments wherever! And you are good to go. But remember to chew properly. Digestion starts at mastication!

# COWBOY BURGER

Yeeeeeehaaaawwwwww! This recipe was inspired by our good friends The Beefy Boys. These lovely lads from Hereford won Best Burger at Grillstock (British BBQ Championships). I made this burger with them last year and it was a huge hit on the DJ BBQ YouTube channel. Heck, it's got two slices of steak on the dang bun. What's not to like? More meat? Yes please!

---

🔪 **MAKES 2 BURGERS**

🍴 **OUTDOORS** Half & half technique

🍳 **INDOORS** Griddle pan on the hob (stovetop)

You'll also need a cloche or large metal bowl to use as a lid

---

400g (14oz) beef mince (ground beef) (min. 20% fat content)

1 × 200g (7oz) sirloin steak (about 3cm/1½ inches thick)

2 slices of cheese (don't go with burger cheese on this one... the Cowboy Burger deserves better flavour – try a medium cheddar or Monterey Jack)

2 large brioche/demi-brioche burger buns

¼ iceberg lettuce, shredded

2–4 tomato slices

Sea salt and black pepper

### AIOLI

1 whole garlic bulb

75ml (2½fl oz/scant ⅓ cup) olive oil

Squeeze of lemon juice

1 tbsp water

Sea salt

---

First off, let's get the garlic for the aioli roasted. Get a load of coals rocking on your grill or preheat your oven to 180°C (350°F/gas mark 4). Loosely wrap the garlic bulb in foil and chuck it in the oven or nestle it in the coals. Leave it there for an hour until it is soft and oozy. Remove and leave to cool.

Peel four of the cloves and smash the garlic with a knife until super smooth. Scrape it into a bowl and add the rest of the aioli ingredients, and blend together well until smooth and gooey, almost like mayonnaise.

Divide the beef mince into two balls and flatten them into large patties. These will be a bit bigger than the norm so you can go thicker. Season with salt and pepper.

Season the steak with salt only and get ready to do some major grilling.

Place the burgers and steak on the grill over direct heat, or on the griddle pan over a high heat on the hob. There are two major beefy foodstuffs cooking now, so you'll need to pay attention. Keep the steak moving so that you can render the fat and build up a nice crust. If you're cooking outdoors, the meat might stick to the grill – don't worry, the grill will release the meat when it's ready. Cook for 1–2 minutes, then flip, and repeat the process until the steaks and burgers are almost cooked exactly how you like them.

*Recipe continues...*

*Recipe continued from page 80.*

Sirloin is best served somewhere between rare and medium rare, and burgers medium. Use a temperature probe to make sure the meat is perfectly cooked – check the internal meat temperatures on page 16.

However, remember the steak will keep cooking while it rests – so pull it off slightly early. And you want to get the cheese on just before the burgers are perfectly cooked – after about 8 minutes for medium. Add the cheese slices on top of each burger and cover with a cloche or big metal bowl to speed up the melt on the cheese.

Let the steak rest while you build the burger. The steak slices are the last addition.

Toast your buns. Lay them out and spread that aioli garlicky goodness onto the bottom bun, followed by the shredded lettuce, cheeseburger, tomato slices and top bun.

Slice the steak lengthways across the grain, then lay two slices across each other to form an 'X' on top of each bun. A cocktail stick might be your friend here – you need something to keep this bad boy from falling apart.

Now play 'Cowboy Song' by Thin Lizzy and feast upon one super-delicious, decadent burger. Wear a Stetson cowboy hat and make these for family and friends. They'll beg you for more! They are that impressive… as is your cowboy hat.

# THE WORLD'S <u>BEST</u> SLOPPY JOE BURGER IN THE HISTORY OF THE WORLD

I grew up on Loose Meat Sandwiches and Sloppy Joes. My father is from Sioux City, Iowa, where this sandwich began life. My dad's side of the family are up at Lake Okoboji in Iowa right now for the yearly family reunion. And it wouldn't be a reunion without a visit to Tastee Inn & Out for one of their Loose Meat Sandwiches. I spent the majority of my childhood in Gaithersburg, Maryland, and the school cafeteria had these at least two or three times a month. Sloppy Joes and Pizza Fridays were my fave. The nearest thing the UK has to the Sloppy Joe is Spag Bol on Toast. Pretty much the same thing... loose beef mince in a tomato sauce.

>  **MAKES 6–8 BURGERS**
>  **OUTDOORS** Half & half technique, saucepan
> **INDOORS** Saucepan on the hob (stovetop)

500g (1lb 2oz) beef mince (ground beef), turkey or pork work too
Olive oil or vegetable oil, for frying
1 medium onion, finely chopped
2 garlic cloves, chopped
1 tbsp tomato purée (paste)
1 × 400g (14oz) can chopped tomatoes
1 tsp dried oregano
1 tbsp brown sugar
Splash of Worcestershire sauce
1 tbsp cider vinegar or white wine vinegar
1 tbsp English mustard
½ beef or veg stock cube, to crumble in
Sea salt and black pepper
6–8 soft white buns
Pickles, sliced (optional)

Get your mince out of the fridge. Then heat up a large saucepan – either over direct heat on the grill, or on a medium/high heat on the hob.

Drizzle some oil into the pan, then fry off your meat until the beef is brown. Remove the beef from the pan and set aside in a bowl. Add a little more oil to the pan if needed and sauté the onion and garlic until softened.

Now add the beef back in with the rest of the ingredients. Slowly stir and cook on a simmer for at the very least 20 minutes. The longer you cook this the better. Also, Sloppy Joe sandwiches always taste better the next day, so you could batch-cook loads and eat it through the week, or even freeze some for another time.

Spoon your tasty filling onto the bottom bun, top with a pickle and the bun lid. Sloppy Joes work well when the meat isn't piled on too thick, as the wetness can overcome the bun and destroy it before you have finished. Less is more in the Sloppy Joe bun. Although I never listen to this advice... I always want more, as you can see.

# MONTY IN THE MIDDLE

This cheeseburger with hidden cheese was inspired by the legendary Juicy Lucy Burger made famous in Minneapolis, Minnesota. There are two bars that claim to have invented it: Matt's Bar and the 5–8 Club. Both joints are within 3 miles of each other. The 5–8 Club version has several different options on cheese, while the Matt's Bar version only offers American. Go ahead and experiment but I only use Monterey Jack cheese. Hence the name, Monty in the Middle. Get it?

---

✎ **MAKES 2 BURGERS**

🍴 **OUTDOORS** Half & half technique, with a frying pan

📅 **INDOORS** Frying pan and griddle pan on the hob (stovetop)

---

500g (1lb 2oz) beef mince (ground beef)
50g Monterey Jack cheese, grated (shredded)
Knob of butter or a little vegetable oil
1 medium onion, sliced
2 brioche burger buns
6 pickle slices (chilli pickle is good with this burger)
Favourite condiments (mayo, ketchup and American yellow mustard)
Sea salt and black pepper

Divide the beef mince into four balls and flatten into thin patties. This will take some expert hand moulding – the thinner the better as you need to get heat to the middle of these burgers so the cheese melts.

Next, lay out the patties and make sure they are equal in size. Place the grated Monterey Jack cheese in the middle of two patties. Make sure that the cheese doesn't touch the edges as the beef mince will need to seal round the outside properly. Place the naked beef patties on top of the cheese patties.

Using your thumb, press along the edges so that you seal the cheese inside. You are basically crimping the outside of the beef patties so that they hold together. It doesn't matter if a little cheese oozes out during the cook. Heck, it looks sexy and any little air holes help to cook the cheese. Season the patties with salt and pepper and set them aside.

Now get your onions rocking. Place a small frying pan over indirect heat on the grill, or if you're indoors, on a low heat on the hob. Stick the knob of butter or some oil in the pan. Once hot, chuck in your onions and cook until they are golden and amazing – around 10 minutes.

You'll need a medium to high heat to cook the Monty in the Middle patties – hot enough to create a crust and melt the cheese but not burn the outside. If you're cooking outdoors, put the patties direct on the grill, or inside use your griddle pan on the hob. These take a bit more

time to cook than a regular burger because of the cheese inside the patty – about 10 minutes in total. They need to be cooked all the way so that the centre goes molten! You wanna create a cheesecano so when ya bite into your burger, the cheese erupts into a delicious gooey mess. Yes!

Toast your buns and add any condiment you like on the bottoms (usually mayo).

Place the patties on the bottom buns straight off the grill. Top with the pickle slices and golden onions and the rest of your favourite condiments, then the lid.

Indulge and make sure you have a napkin and a cold beer handy, to keep your mouth clean and cool. Congrats, you just paid honour to the almighty Juicy Lucy with your own, Monty in the Middle.

# THE SMASHED BURGER

The Smashed Burger is a classic and has been made in restaurants all over the planet. If I'm with T-Bone and we see the 'smashing' technique going down in an eating establishment, it's easy – 'We'll have that!' T-Bone and I both have kids (he has one son and I have three boys) and this is a great recipe to make with your kids. Children love smashing stuff – and here you get to smash stuff *and* eat it. And the smashing makes it taste better! There's some cool stuff happening in this recipe, so pay attention. Now, gather the kids and get smashing.

---

🍴 **MAKES 4 BURGERS**

🍖 **OUTDOORS** Half & half technique, with a frying pan or plancha

🔥 **INDOORS** Frying pan on the hob (stovetop)

You'll also need a cloche or large metal bowl to use as a lid. And something strong, metal and flat to smash with, a metal spatula would work, or the base of a frying pan

---

400g (14oz) beef mince (ground beef)
American yellow mustard
4 slices of burger cheese
4 burger buns
Water in a jug or squeezy bottle
Favourite condiments (mayo and ketchup, basically – because the mustard is cooked in)
¼ iceberg lettuce, shredded
Sea salt and black pepper

Divide the beef mince into four balls and roll into perfect spheres of awesomeness. If you're cooking outdoors, place your frying pan or plancha over direct heat and make sure it's hot. Indoors, get your frying pan really hot over a high heat on the hob.

Now throw your balls of meat down onto your hot frying pan or plancha and smash them into flat patties with a strong metal spatula.

If you want to get more weight on the beef, try using the base of another frying pan. You're not looking for perfection though – you want imperfect-looking patties with lots of lovely nooks and crannies resulting in fjords of flavour. Season with salt and pepper.

Have your American yellow mustard ready in a bowl with a basting brush.

You want to sear the bottom of the patties and get a nice crust (around 2–3 minutes), then flip them over and brush on some of the mustard.

When the other side has developed a crust (after another 2–3 minutes), flip the burger again and brush on more mustard. Give the burger a couple of flips until the mustard is cooked into the patty.

*Recipes continues...*

*Recipe continued from page 88.*

These burgers are best served medium. When they're almost cooked – after about 8 minutes – add the cheese slices on top of each burger and cover with a cloche or metal bowl to speed up the melt on the cheese. Use a temperature probe to make sure the burgers are perfectly cooked – check the internal meat temperatures on page 16 – then grab your water jug!

This next bit is the key to making this the best burger ever. Our good friends The Beefy Boys use this technique on every single burger they serve. Those dudes won second place in Best Burger at the World Food Championships in Vegas a couple of years back. If it works for them, it's gonna work for you.

Place the top burger bun onto the cheese and then add a splash of water next to the burger and quickly replace the cloche. This creates a lovely steam that will make the burger nice and squishy. You only need to leave the cloche on for 15–30 seconds to achieve the ultimate steamy squishiness.

While you wait, get that bottom bun ready with a splodge of mayo (or your favourite condiment) and a handful of lettuce. Then throw the rest of the burger on top and you are ready to indulge in this tastiest of burgers.

# SUPER-DUPER TRIPLY AGED BEEF BURGER OF DECADENCE

If you think you have had a really rich burger before, it will have to have owned an island and a few fast cars to beat this one! This burger will make you realize just how rich burgers can be – everything is aged in some way to really bring out that glorious rich flavour. This is deep, unrelenting, super-tasty, beefy beefness!

---

🔪 **MAKES 2 BURGERS**

🍖 **OUTDOORS** Half & half technique, with an optional plancha or frying pan

🍳 **INDOORS** Griddle or frying pan on the hob (stovetop)

You'll also need a cloche or metal bowl to use as a lid

---

400g (14oz) beef mince (ground beef) (min. 20% fat content; at least 50-day dry-aged)
4 slices of well-aged pancetta
4 slices of aged cheese or super mature cheddar
2 seeded burger buns
Sea salt and black pepper

### TOMATOES
60g (2¼oz) sun-dried tomatoes
50ml (1¾fl oz/scant ¼ cup) light soy sauce

### HEAVY METAL BLACK GARLIC MAYO
2 tbsp mayonnaise
4 black garlic cloves, crushed
¼ tsp English mustard

### SAUERKRAUT
100g (3½oz) sauerkraut
2 tbsp freshly grated horseradish
Dash of lemon juice

Divide the mince into two balls and hand-press into patties, so there is a nice rough outer edge. Leave to rest in the fridge while you make the rest of the components.

Drizzle the sun-dried tomatoes with soy sauce and leave on a cleaned sword (or somewhere similar) to marinate for 10 minutes.

Make the Black Garlic Mayo by mixing all the ingredients up with a whisk, until you have a smooth Iron Maiden-style sauce! Set aside.

Mix the sauerkraut with the horseradish and lemon juice, and set aside.

Get your grill nice and hot, or if you're cooking indoors set your griddle or frying pan over a high heat on the hob. Season your patties with salt and pepper, then get cooking – you want to grill or griddle your pancetta alongside the burgers.

If you're cooking outdoors, the meat might stick to the grill. You can use a plancha or frying pan if you prefer, but don't worry – the grill will release the meat when it's ready. Cook for 2–3 minutes, then flip, and repeat the process until the patties have a nice crust and are almost cooked – about 8 minutes in total.

Add the cheese slices on top and cover with a cloche or metal lid to speed up the melt. Use a temperature probe to make sure the burger is perfectly cooked – check the internal meat temperatures on page 16 – then remove your burgers and the pancetta. Keep it all warm while you toast the buns.

Now get ready to put this most grand-daddy
of burgers together. Layer up your buns with a
symphony of sauerkraut, crispy aged pancetta,
rich beef, aged cheese, heavy metal mayo and old
sun-dried tomatoes!

You are the single bestest burger-creator of
the last 30 minutes on this planet called Earth.
Congrats. Man, how are we gonna top this one?
Well, turn the page my friend!

# WORLD CHAMPION BURGER

We served up BBQ and burgers for five years at the British BBQ Championships, Grillstock. Our friends The Beefy Boys create award-winning burgers. Their secret weapon: rib eye. They rolled up to a butcher and asked him to mince (grind) a load of beautiful dry-aged rib eye... lots of it. At first, the butcher refused, saying 'Why would you do that?' He eventually did what they asked and The Beefy Boys now have a world-class burger! That's why.

🔪 **MAKES 4 BURGERS**

🍴 **OUTDOORS** Half & half technique, plus a plancha

🔲 **INDOORS** Oven, plus frying pan and griddle pan on the hob (stovetop)

You'll also need a cloche or large metal bowl to use as a lid

250g (9oz) brisket
250g (9oz) dry-aged rib eye steak, minced (ground)
1 tbsp butter
1 red onion, finely sliced
1 tbsp brown sugar
4 slices of aged Gouda cheese
4 seeded burger buns
Few leaves of little gem lettuce
1 beef tomato, sliced
Sea salt and black pepper

**SMOKED GARLIC MAYO**
1 whole garlic bulb
100g (3½oz) mayonnaise
Juice of 1 lemon

First, shape up the most expensive beef burgers you're ever likely to make. Divide the mince into four balls and flatten into patties. Set aside.

Put your garlic on to smoke – the best way is popping the bulb into a proper smoker and leaving it for about 2 hours. If you can't smoke your garlic outdoors, just wrap it in a little foil and leave it in the oven for about an hour (at around 180°C/350°F/gas mark 4). When the garlic is cooked, peel and crush it. Add it to the mayonnaise, along with the lemon juice, and whisk it together.

Set your plancha over direct heat and get it nice and hot, or put a frying pan over a medium heat on the hob. Throw in the butter and get it foaming. When it starts to turn brown, add the sliced red onions and sugar. Keep stirring for about 4–5 minutes until they are golden and sweet. Set aside.

Get your grill nice and hot, or set your griddle pan over a high heat on the hob. Take your indulgent rib eye patties, season well with salt and pepper and get them on the grill, plancha or griddle. Now remember, these are bloody expensive burgers so don't screw this up!

*Recipe continues...*

*Recipe continued from page 95.*

If you're cooking straight on the grill, the meat might stick – don't worry, relax, the grill will release the meat when it's ready. Cook for 1–2 minutes, then flip, and repeat the process until they are almost done.

These burgers are best served medium rare. When they're almost cooked – after about 5 minutes – add the cheese slices on top of each burger and cover with a cloche or metal bowl to speed up the melt on the cheese (it'll take max 30 seconds this way). Use a temperature probe to make sure the burger is perfectly cooked – check the internal meat temperatures on page 16 – then remove your burgers and keep warm while you toast the buns.

Spread the bottom bun with a thick dollop of garlic mayo, layer up the lettuce and cheesy steak burger, followed by the caramelized onions and tomato slice. Finish with the top bun and present your challenger in front of the world!

# FLEETWOOD MAC & CHEESE BURGER

Everyone likes Mac & Cheese, and everyone likes a cheeseburger. AND, everyone likes Fleetwood Mac. I really need to see them before they stop touring. I did get the chance to see Stevie Nicks open for Tom Petty a couple of summers back in London. That was awesome. They teamed up for 'Stop Draggin' My Heart Around' and my life was complete! This is a pretty quick and easy Mac & Cheese recipe. (Saying that, I always have a couple of boxes of Kraft's Macaroni & Cheese in the cupboard. My boys love it – it's like crack for kids!)

---

🔧 **MAKES 4 BURGERS**

🍴 **OUTDOORS** Half & half technique, with a saucepan and plancha; not recommended for the frickles

🔥 **INDOORS** Saucepan and large frying pan on the hob (stovetop)

You'll also need a deep-fat fryer or deep saucepan

---

500g (1lb 2oz) beef mince (ground beef)
Knob of butter or a little vegetable oil
4 burger buns
Ketchup
Sea salt and black pepper

## MAC & CHEESE
175g (6oz) macaroni
200g (7oz) red Leicester or cheddar cheese, grated (shredded)
25g (¾oz) butter
1 tbsp English mustard

There's a lot of prep here. So, here's what you do: make the mac & cheese, make the frickles, make the burgers, put them together, add some ketchup and eat. Nice work. We are outta here!

Alright, do y'all wanna know how to do this thang? Let's do it!

The mac & cheese needs to be made at least an hour in advance. It's best to make it the night before or at least the morning of the cook, as you need to refrigerate it so it's easier to shape and holds together well.

Cook the macaroni according to the instructions on the packet – either over a high heat on the hob or over direct heat on the grill. When the pasta is drained, immediately add the grated cheese, butter and mustard, and season with salt and pepper. Mix thoroughly until it has a smooth consistency... like the boxed Kraft stuff. Then chill it! Throw that cheesy pasta gooeyness into the refrigerator.

Now it's frickle time. Pour the oil into a large, deep saucepan (or you can use a deep-fat fryer), set it over a high heat and get that oil hot. Once the temperature reaches 180°C (350°F), you are good to fry.

*Ingredients and recipe continue...*

## FRICKLES

Vegetable oil, for deep-fat frying (at least 2 litres/3½ pints)

100g (3½oz/¾ cup) self-raising (self-rising) flour, plus extra for dusting

175ml (6fl oz) lager or sparkling water

Jar of sliced pickles (dill is better than sweet for that extra tang)

*Recipe continued from page 98.*

Whisk the flour and beer or water together in a mixing bowl, then season well. Dust the pickles with flour. The easiest way is to tip the flour out into a small roasting tin (pan) and throw in the pickles until they are lightly covered in flour. Dip the floured pickles into the batter and carefully lower them into the pan or deep-fat fryer and cook till golden. This will usually take 3–4 minutes. Remove and lay on paper towels to drain.

Now it's time to make the burgers. Get your cooking surface nice and hot – either sit your plancha over direct heat on the grill or your frying pan over a high heat on the hob.

Divide the beef mince into four balls and flatten them into patties. Season with salt and pepper and throw them in the frying pan or plancha. If you're cooking outdoors directly on the grill, the meat might stick – don't worry, the grill will release the meat when it's ready. Cook for 1–2 minutes, then flip, and repeat the process until they are done (about 6 minutes for medium).

Meanwhile, shape the chilled mac & cheese into four patties. Chuck the knob of butter or a glug of vegetable oil onto your cooking surface – plancha or frying pan set over a medium-hot heat (or less direct heat on the grill). When the fat is melted, carefully place your mac & cheese patties onto the cooking surface. You might need to cook them in two batches, if you don't have enough room. Fry until you have a nice brown crust (about 2 minutes), then very carefully flip and cook until the other side has a nice crust.

Use a temperature probe to make sure the burger is perfectly cooked – check the internal meat temperatures on page 16 – then remove your burgers and keep warm while you toast the buns.

When toasted, on the bottom bun add the meat patty, fried mac & cheese, a dollop of ketchup, the frickles and the top toasted bun. That was a bit of work, but how good is that burger? You rule!

# WHO NEEDS
# RED MEAT?

# TUNA MELT BURGER

What's better than a tuna melt? Nothing! Actually, hold the mayo, a tuna melt in a burger! Tuna melts should be burgers! They are usually served open faced or in long ciabatta buns. Cut those buns in half and you got yourself a burger bun. You can find some burger-size ciabatta buns in your supermarket. If not, use a sourdough bun. But wait, what's the perfect way to make tuna mayo? Well, in the immortal words of Michael Keaton in one of his earliest films, *Night Shift*: 'What if you mix mayonnaise right in the can with the tuna fish? Hold it! Hold it! Wait a minute! Chuck! [Henry Winkler fresh from playing the Fonz on *Happy Days*]! Take live tuna fish and *feed* them mayonnaise. Oh, this is good [speaks into tape recorder]. Call StarKist! [popular brand of canned Tuna in the USA].' Watch the film! It's also got Shelley Long from the hit show *Cheers* in it.

✎ **MAKES 3 OR 4 BURGERS, DEPENDING ON HOW HUNGRY YOU ARE**

🍖 **OUTDOORS** Kettle-style grill with lid, half & half technique, with a baking sheet

🎛 **INDOORS** Oven, with a baking sheet

You'll also need a cloche or large metal bowl to use as a lid if you're cooking outdoors

4 ciabatta or sourdough buns
2 spring onions (scallions), sliced
2 red chillies, deseeded and chopped
150g (5oz) canned tuna (1 regular can), drained
2 heaped tbsp mayonnaise
Dash of Worcestershire sauce
Pinch of cayenne pepper
175g (6oz) cheese of your choice, grated (shredded)
Sea salt and black pepper

Preheat your oven to 220°C (425°F/gas mark 7) or get your outdoor grill rocking.

Cut your buns in half, and reserve some of the spring onions and chillies for garnishing. Take the rest of your ingredients, apart from the cheese, and cast into a large mixing bowl and stir until you've reached a nice sloppy creamy chunky tuna mulch. Mmmmmm... that's mulchy.

Toast your buns and build right on the baking sheet you're going to cook them on. Spoon your tuna mayo mulch onto the base, then cover with cheese and top with the remaining slices of spring onions and chillies. Throw some cracked pepper and salt on top.

Chuck the baking sheet in the oven or outdoor grill and wait till the cheese has melted. Outdoors, you'll need a lid or a cloche. This can take anywhere from 10 to 20 minutes, depending on how far you wanna take the cheese. I like it on the right side of burnt like a leopard-skin coat.

If you've got kids, this is a perfect, quick and easy cook. They love 'em!

# WINGMANS KOREAN BURGER: SEOULJA BOI

Wingmans makes the best chicken wings in the UK. London Wing Fest is the biggest chicken wing festival in all of Europe, and Ben and David from Wingmans have won trophies every year. In 2018, they won three: Judge's Choice Award for Best Buffalo Wing, and two People's Choice Awards for Best Buffalo Wing and Best Wild Wing. This is a version of their winning Wild Wing recipe – it's a big one, but worth the effort! And if you are ever in London, go pay the boys a visit in Kilburn.

 **MAKES 4 BURGERS**

**OUTDOORS** Not recommended

**INDOORS** Saucepan, griddle pan and frying pan on the hob (stovetop), plus deep-fat fryer or deep saucepan

**PANKO CHICKEN**

4 chicken thighs (boneless and skinless)
100g (3½oz/¾ cup) plain (all-purpose) flour
1 tsp garlic granules
1 tsp onion granules
1 tsp ground coriander
1 tsp ground white pepper
1 tsp ground black pepper
2 tsp table salt
2 eggs, beaten
250g (9oz) panko breadcrumbs
1 tsp dried oregano
Vegetable oil, for deep-fat frying (at least 2 litres/3½ pints)

Trim off all the excess fat, sinew and gristle from the chicken thighs, and set aside.

Set out three shallow bowls. In the first one, place the flour, garlic and onion granules, coriander, both the peppers and half the salt. Add the beaten eggs into the second bowl. Finally, put the panko breadcrumbs, with the remaining 1 teaspoon of salt and the dried oregano, into the third bowl.

Coat the thighs in the flour, then the egg, and then the breadcrumbs, making sure to press the crumbs into the chicken. If you're not cooking this up straight away, keep the coated chicken chilled until ready to cook.

Next make the sauce for the coating. Put the gochujang, sesame oil, cider vinegar, sugar, black beans and both soy sauces into a saucepan set over a low heat. Bring up to a simmer and turn off. If it's too thick to mix, add a splash of water. Add the garlic and black sesame seeds and whisk together. Set aside.

For the sesame mayo, toast the sesame seeds in a dry frying pan until just beginning to turn golden – 2 or 3 minutes – and let them cool. Mix with the Kewpie mayo, sesame oil, salt and lime juice. Set aside.

*Ingredients and recipe continue...*

## SAUCE FOR COATING

250g (9oz/generous 1 cup) gochujang (red chilli paste)
50ml (1¾fl oz/scant ¼ cup) sesame oil
200ml (7fl oz/generous ¾ cup) cider vinegar
150g (5½oz/¾ cup) caster (superfine) sugar
100g (3½oz) fermented black beans
25ml (scant 1 fl oz/1⅔ tbsp) light soy sauce
25ml (scant 1 fl oz/1⅔ tbsp) dark soy sauce
1 tbsp garlic granules
30g (1oz/3¾ tbsp) black sesame seeds

## TOASTED SESAME MAYO

100g (3½oz) white sesame seeds
200g (7oz/scant 1 cup) Kewpie Mayonnaise
1 tsp sesame oil
1 tsp sea salt
Juice of ½ lime

## GRILLED PINEAPPLE

½ small pineapple, peeled and cut into 0.5cm (¼-inch) thick steaks

## PICKLED CUCUMBER

½ cucumber
50ml (1¾fl oz/¼ cup) ponzu (citrus soy sauce)
1 tsp black sesame seeds
Handful of coriander (cilantro), chopped
25g (¾oz/2 tbsp) caster (superfine) sugar
1 tsp sesame oil

## GARNISH

Iceberg lettuce, shredded
2 spring onions (scallions), sliced
½ red onion, thinly sliced
1 red chilli, thinly sliced

## BUN

4 brioche buns
Knob of butter, melted

*Recipe continued from page 107.*

Get a griddle pan nice and hot over a medium to high heat on the hob. Add the pineapple slices to the pan and allow to colour and char slightly (it'll take about 3 or 4 minutes per side) before removing and setting to the side.

For the pickled cucumber, use a swivel peeler to slice thin ribbons off your cucumber and place in a bowl. Mix the ponzu, black sesame seeds, coriander, sugar and sesame oil together, and adjust the seasoning if you need to with a touch of salt (or if you like your pickle sweeter add a touch more sugar). Pour the dressing over the cucumber, stir, then keep chilled.

Pour the oil into a large saucepan (or you can use a deep-fat fryer), set it over a high heat and get that oil hot. Make sure your garnishes are all prepared, and get ready to fry! Once the temperature reaches 180°C (350°F), you are good to go.

Deep-fry the chicken thighs for 7 or 8 minutes, or until the core temperature reaches at least 75°C (167°F).

Toast the brioche buns and brush the inside of the top and bottom with the melted butter.

Now, build that burger. Spread the bottom bun with sesame mayo and add some iceberg lettuce. Dip the cooked chicken into the sauce until completely coated, then place on top of the lettuce. Top with grilled pineapple, followed by ribbons of pickled cucumber (make sure you get the coriander and sesame seeds in there), and a sprinkling of spring onions, red onion and chilli. Spread the top bun with more sesame mayo, then bang it on and enjoy.

# DJ BBQ'S BUFFALO CAULIFLOWER BURGER

Cauliflower is so hot right now... and even hotter when you cover it in DJ BBQ Hot Sauce (page 162). I love buffalo wings and I love cauliflower, so it makes sense to put 'em together into one veggie recipe. And the results are as magical as Harry Potter! By the way, my friend, Tim, ripped the last page of the last Potter book and ate it in front of me so I couldn't finish it. It was a first edition as well. Dick!

**MAKES 2 BURGERS**

 **OUTDOORS** Not recommended

 **INDOORS** Saucepan on the hob (stovetop), plus deep-fat fryer or deep saucepan

Vegetable oil, for deep-fat frying (at least 2 litres/3½ pints)
100g (3½oz) butter
150ml (5fl oz/⅔ cup) water
1 small cauliflower, cut into 2 steaks
150ml (5fl oz/⅔ cup) DJ BBQ Hot Sauce (see page 162)
200g (7oz/1⅔ cups) self-raising (self-rising) flour
1 tbsp ground cumin
1 tbsp paprika
1 tbsp fine sea salt
150ml (5fl oz/⅔ cup) mayonnaise
50ml (1¾fl oz/scant ¼ cup) full-fat (whole) milk
50ml (1¾fl oz/scant ¼ cup) cider vinegar
25g (¾oz) blue cheese, crumbled

**TO SERVE**
2 large soft buns
Lettuce, shredded
Pickles, sliced

Put the butter and water into a medium saucepan over a medium heat and bring to the boil. Add the cauliflower and simmer the steaks, turning every now and then, until the water has evaporated and the cauliflower is almost cooked through. Season with salt and leave to drain onto a paper towel.

Add the DJ BBQ Hot Sauce to the remaining butter in the pan and whisk together until smooth – this is your buffalo sauce.

Mix the flour, cumin, paprika and the 1 tablespoon of salt in a large bowl. In another large bowl, whisk the mayo, milk and cider vinegar until smooth.

Place half the mayo mix into another bowl for the blue cheese dressing. Add in the blue cheese and whisk until smooth, then set aside.

Pour the oil into a large saucepan (or you can use a deep-fat fryer), set it over a high heat and get that oil hot. Once the temperature reaches 180°C (350°F), you are good to fry.

Dip each cauliflower steak into the mayo mix (the one without the cheese), then dip into the flour mix, making sure they are fully covered. When the oil is hot, carefully drop the steaks into the oil and cook for 2–3 minutes until golden brown. Drain on a paper towel.

Layer up your buns with the cauliflower steak, then lettuce, buffalo sauce, and then add some blue cheese dressing to bring even more awesomeness – this will appease both your veggie friends and your meat-eating brethren!

# BEETROOT BLOODY BEETROOT

Sepultura's anthem 'Roots Bloody Roots' inspired this – the most metal veggie burger I could get my charcoal-encrusted hands on! This burger is unlike most veggie burgers as it's the colour of human blood! AHH-HAHAHHAHAHAHHAHAHA (evil laugh)! This burger is also made to be really moist and really smoky, leaving you wanting more and more and more!

**MAKES 4 BURGERS**

**OUTDOORS** Half & half technique, with a frying pan, plus veg cooked dirty on coals

**INDOORS** Oven, plus frying pan on the hob (stovetop)

## PATTIES

1 onion
1 whole garlic bulb
2 corn on the cobs (or 200g/
    7oz canned sweetcorn/
    whole-kernel corn)
1 × 400g (14oz) can butter
    beans, drained and dried out
    on paper towels
2 beetroot (beets), cooked,
    peeled and grated
2 tbsp plain (all-purpose) flour
Pinch of dried oregano
1 tsp celery salt
1 tsp black pepper
Juice of ½ lemon
Vegetable oil, for frying

## SPICE MIX

2 tbsp plain (all-purpose) flour
2 tsp paprika
2 tsp cayenne pepper
2 tsp sea salt
2 tsp black pepper
2 tsp garlic granules
2 tsp onion granules

Get your coals cooking or preheat your oven to 200°C (400°F/gas mark 6).

If you're cooking outdoors, get your onion and garlic dirty by roasting them whole in the bed of coals. Nestle them directly in among the coals and turn every so often for at least 1 hour –you want them black all over and soft. If you're indoors, put them on a baking sheet in the oven and roast until burnt and soft.

Now do the same with the corn on the cobs, but for only 2 minutes on each side, until they are charred all over. If indoors, you can do this on the griddle pan. Leave all the veg to cool for at least 30 minutes.

While the vegetables are cooking/cooling, mix together the flour and all the spices for the spice mix. Then take half of this spice mix and place in a shallow bowl.

When the veg is cool, get yourself a big wooden board. This will be your chopping board and bowl in one! Peel the onion and finely chop the cooked insides on the board. Squeeze four of the cooked garlic cloves out of their skins and onto the board. Slice the kernels off the corn cobs and add to the board with the onion and garlic. Also add the drained beans, grated beetroot, flour, oregano, celery salt, black pepper and the lemon juice, as well as the other half of the spice mix.

Using a sharp knife, smash everything together on the board like you're in a mosh pit at a Sepultura gig. The mix will be quite wet but this means your burger will be perfectly moist. Divide your mixture into four, and mould yourself some patties.

**TO SERVE**
4 brioche buns
2 butterhead lettuce leaves
1 tomato, sliced
Ketchup
Mayonnaise

Add some oil to a frying pan and set it over a medium heat on the hob or over the direct heat on the grill. When the oil is hot, coat the patties in the spicy flour mix and carefully place each one in the pan and cook until you have a nice crust (about 2–3 minutes per side). Don't have the heat too high, otherwise you will burn your patties and your self-respect. Turn when you have a good crust, and repeat once more on each side until the patties hold together and look amazeballs.

When the burgers are ready, toast your buns and serve as you like it with lettuce, tomato, ketchup and mayo.

# SMOKED HADDOCK BURGER

Smoked haddock is one of the UK's most cracking of fishy ingredients. If you can't find it in the shop, you can always go sea fishing, catch a beautiful haddock, bring it home, gut it, scale it, fillet it, brine it and cold-smoke it yourself! Orrrrr, just buy a similar smoked white fish from the supermarket or fishmonger. This goes so well with crispy samphire, which is as salty and more-ish as the fish itself.

---

✎ **MAKES 2 BURGERS**

🍴 **OUTDOORS** Half & half technique, with a saucepan for the fish; not recommended for the samphire

📱 **INDOORS** Saucepan on the hob (stovetop), plus deep-fat fryer or deep saucepan

---

Vegetable oil, for deep-fat frying (at least 2 litres/3½ pints)
2 white poppyseed buns

### SMOKED HADDOCK
1 litre (35fl oz/4¼ cups) milk
2 bay leaves
2 garlic cloves, crushed
8 peppercorns
½ tsp salt
2 × 250g (9oz) thick skinless smoked haddock fillets

### SAMPHIRE
100g (3½oz/scant 1 cup) gram flour
130ml (4½fl oz/generous ½ cup) water
Pinch of salt
200g (7oz) samphire

### CITRUS MAYO
Zest of 1 lemon
Zest and juice of 1 lime
2 tbsp mayonnaise

First, pour yourself a pint of awesome and put on your best kilt.

Then make the citrus mayo by mixing all the ingredients together well. Set aside to infuse.

Put the milk in a saucepan, with the bay leaves, garlic, peppercorns and salt, and bring up to a simmer – either over direct heat on the grill or over a medium to low heat on the hob. Add the fish and gently poach for 5 minutes. Remove onto a plate and set aside to rest for a few minutes.

Pour the oil into a large saucepan (or you can use a deep-fat fryer), set it over a high heat and get that oil hot. Once the temperature reaches 180°C (350°F), you are good to fry.

Whisk up the gram flour and water with a pinch of salt. Add in the samphire, mix again so it is all covered, then sprinkle the coated samphire into the fryer so it doesn't all stick together. Remove when crispy (about 3 minutes) and drain on paper towels.

Toast your buns and stuff them with the crispy samphire and poached fish, topped with a big dollop of the citrus mayo. Cracking!

# KAKIAGE BURGER

This more-ish burger is a killer creation that was inspired by Scott Hallsworth while we were actually shooting his burger (Chicken-fried Chicken Burger on page 150). It's a great vegetarian recipe and so delicious with the crunchiness of the batter, the mega power of the veg, a double-fry technique and the super-soy BBQ sauce.

 **MAKES 2 BURGERS**

**OUTDOORS** Not recommended

**INDOORS** Frying pan on the hob (stovetop), plus deep-fat fryer or deep saucepan

1 corn on the cob
1 small white onion, thinly sliced
2 spring onions (scallions), thinly sliced, plus extra for garnishing
150g (5½oz) tenderstem broccoli, roughly chopped
1 medium carrot, grated
75g (2¾oz) sweet potato, peeled and grated
10g (2 tsp) table salt
Vegetable oil, for deep-fat frying (at least 2 litres/3½ pints), plus 100ml (3½fl oz/scant ½ cup) for frying
2 charcoal buns

**TEMPURA BATTER**
60g (2½oz/½oz cup) plain flour
20g (¾oz) rice flour
pinch of salt
200ml (6¾fl oz) ice cold sparkling water

**SOY BBQ SAUCE**
3 tbsp BBQ sauce
2 tbsp light soy sauce
2–3 tbsp water

Slice the kernels off your corn on the cob and chuck into a colander, along with all the other prepared veg and the salt. Place the colander over a bowl and leave for 10 minutes.

To make up the batter mix, grab a large bowl, and mix all the dry ingredients together. Pour in the ice cold water and roughly stir until just combined, try not to over-stir, as you will probably end up displeased with a rubbery, rather than crispy, finish.

Pour the 100ml of vegetable oil into the hot frying pan and allow to heat up on a high heat.

Then pour the oil for deep-fat frying into a large saucepan (or you can use a deep-fat fryer), set it over a high heat and get that oil hot. Once the temperature reaches 180°C (350°F), you are good to fry.

When the oils in both the frying pan and the fryer are hot, grab half of that beautiful veg and dip into the batter mix, give it a good squeeze together to make a single patty.

Next, carefully place into the hot frying pan. Repeat with the remaining veg for a second patty. Leave to fry until they form a crust so they hold together (a matter of 2 minutes per side), then remove, quickly dip back into the batter and straight into the deep-fat fryer to cook for 4–5 minutes until golden brown.

*Recipe continues...*

*Recipe continued from page 116.*

This double fry will give an ultra-crispy batter coating for your tempura burgers. Drain on paper towels and start dreaming of your soy BBQ sauce!

Toast your buns. Do try charcoal buns made from coconut ash if you can find them – they look and taste sooooooo good... almost as good as Morley's chicken in Wandsworth, London!

Damn that place is good! After doing the last shoot for the book, me and Foragey Dave (see Tippy Taco Burger, page 124) went to Morley's for some awesome fried chicken wings. Their batter is so spicy and awesome! Anyway, on the way back home we were hooning it on our long boards down the road when Dave tried to power-slide over some crossing nipples and stacked it like a toddler slipping over in the bath! I could only see the funny side, as he slammed his elbows and knees into the rock-hard concrete shouting things like 'Aaaaaahhhh, I don't wanna smash in my perfect nose!...'

Anyway! When your buns are toasted, quickly mix together the BBQ sauce, soy sauce and enough water to thin it down a bit. Load up the kakiage burgers onto the bun bottoms, top with spring onions and pour a generous amount of the soy BBQ sauce over everything, then finish with the bun top. Dig in!

# GRILLED INDIAN LOBSTER ROLL

This cracking (get it... lobster shell!) recipe is inspired by one of my favourite dishes and photos from my *Fire Food* book (Dirty Loaded Lobster Rolls). Here I've decided to make it even more special with a curry sauce. The sauce can be made ahead of time and just pulled out whenever a lobster comes knocking at your door!

🔪 **MAKES 4 BURGERS**

🍴 **OUTDOORS** Half & half technique, with a frying pan

📦 **INDOORS** Grill, plus a frying pan on the hob (stovetop)

2 live medium-sized lobsters, killed humanely and halved lengthways
4 white poppyseed rolls
Handful of fresh coriander (cilantro), chopped

**SAUCE FOR THE LOBSTER**
Vegetable oil, for frying
1 red onion, finely chopped
1 red chilli, deseeded and chopped
2 tsp garlic paste
2 tsp ginger paste
2 tsp ground coriander
1 tsp black pepper
½ tsp ground turmeric
Pinch of chilli flakes (crushed chili pepper)
Pinch of ground cloves
2 tbsp toasted desiccated coconut
100ml (3½fl oz/½ cup) passata
200ml (7fl oz/¾ cup) coconut milk

**YOGURT SAUCE**
200g (7oz/¾ cup) thick natural (plain) yoghurt
Zest of 2 limes
Few sprigs of mint

If you're cooking outdoors, get your grill rocking. Indoors, get the grill on your oven nice and hot.

Then make the sauce for the lobster. Heat up a frying pan – either over direct heat on the grill or over a low to medium heat on the hob. Add some oil and slowly fry off the onion and chilli, for 10 minutes until golden. Add in the garlic, ginger and spices, and cook gently for another 5 minutes. Add in the coconut, passata and coconut milk, and cook for another 15–20 minutes until rich and thick. Add a little water if it starts to catch.

Next make the yogurt sauce. Mix the yogurt with the lime and mint, and set aside.

Cook your lobster, shell side facing the heat (either indoors or outdoors), for just 2 minutes. Turn the lobster and cook for another minute on the other side. Rest on a tray. Then carefully remove the half-cooked meat out of the shell and set aside – try to keep it intact.

Heat up your lobster sauce and add the lobster meat. Keep stirring for 2–3 minutes, until the lobster is cooked through.

Toast your rolls and lay them out for this most spicy of builds. Pile the bottom bun with the sliced lobster, spoon the yogurt sauce over the top and finish with some coriander and the bun lid. Get a pint of lager ready – you're gonna need it!

# MOUTH PARTY BURGERS

# TIPPY TACO BURGER

Back when I was a young dorky kid, my momma would take me to the only Mexican restaurant in Gaithersburg, Maryland: Tippy's Taco House. I always went for the classic seasoned ground beef crispy taco with shredded iceberg lettuce, pico de gallo and guac. It was basic but perfect. I really wanted to create a burger that would pay homage to that old-school taco house. So I enlisted the help of our partner in festival cooking, Dave 'Forage Sussex' Fennings, and came up with this killer taco burger.

 **MAKES 4 BURGERS**

**OUTDOORS** Half & half technique, with frying pan

**INDOORS** Frying pan on the hob (stovetop)

### SPICED BEEF
450g (1lb) beef mince (ground beef)
1 red (bell) pepper, deseeded and chopped
1 red onion, finely chopped
1 jalapeño, deseeded and chopped
2 garlic cloves, peeled and chopped
Light olive oil or vegetable oil, for frying (if needed)
½ tsp paprika
Pinch of ground cumin
2 tbsp tomato purée (paste)
Dash of Tabasco sauce
Dash of Worcestershire sauce

### PICO DE GALLO
3 plum (or normal) tomatoes, chopped
1 medium red onion, finely sliced
1 jalapeño, deseeded and finely sliced
Handful of chopped coriander (cilantro)

First, make all the toppings, so it's a quick and easy build at the end. Add all the pico de gallo ingredients into a bowl and mix well.

Slice around the avocados lengthways, cutting all the way to the stone, and pull apart into two halves. Remove the stone with a spoon, then scoop out the flesh into a small bowl. Smash the avocado flesh in the bowl and add the lime and salt. Smash some more. Woohooooo... smashing is fun.

Now, let's get cooking!

Get your frying pan nice and hot – either over direct heat on the grill or over a high heat on the hob – then add the beef mince. Make sure you brown the beef on a high heat. Don't cook the beef at a low temperature, or you'll steam it and it won't taste as good.

Once the meat is browned, use a slotted spoon to transfer it to a bowl, then throw the red pepper, onion, jalapeño and garlic into the beefy frying pan. You should have enough beef fat in the pan to cook your veggies in, but if not you can add some oil.

When the veggies are nice and soft – about 5 minutes – add the browned beef back into the frying pan with the spices, tomato purée, Tabasco and Worcestershire sauce. Mix together, so all those wonderful flavours become one.

Toast your buns, as you'll need a crusty barrier to contain this messy concoction.

Pinch of salt
Juice of ½ lime

**GUACAMOLE**
2 ripe avocados
Juice of 1 lime
1 tsp salt

**TO SERVE**
4 burger buns
¼ iceberg lettuce, shredded
6 radishes, very thinly sliced
Pickled jalapeños (optional)

Here's how ya build this banging taco burger. Lay out the bottom bun and add the shredded lettuce and sliced radishes, followed by the spiced beef mix, guacamole, pico de gallo and pickled jalapeños. If you don't want this burger spicy, then lose the jalapeños. It'll still be amaze-atron. Good luck eating this one. Make sure you have some corn tortillas or corn chips waiting on standby to scoop up the tasty stragglers.

# SURF & TURF BURGER

Surf & turf is usually one of the most expensive items on the menu. Well, this recipe ain't exactly cheap, but it will go a lot further than a pure slab of meat – you can feed up to four people if you don't get too greedy with the ingredients. Boom, a luxury recipe spread out to feed the masses (or you and three of your mates). Let's head to decadent-ville.

 **MAKES 2-4 BURGERS**

**OUTDOORS** Half & half technique, with cast-iron frying pan

**INDOORS** Griddle pan and cast-iron frying pan on the hob (stovetop)

### TURF
2 × 250g (9oz) rib eye steaks (at least 21-day dry-aged)
Sea salt and black pepper

### SURF
75g (2¾oz) butter
Big pinch of saffron
200g (7oz) large peeled tiger prawns (shrimp)
1 tsp sea salt
Large squeeze of lemon juice
1 tsp thyme leaves

### TO SERVE
1 x portion of Beard Hair Chips (see page 160)
2, 3 or 4 awesome seeded buns

Start by getting your steaks out of the fridge for up to 2 hours before you cook them. You can use this time to prep the Beard Hair Chips (see page 160).

Get your grill rocking to a nice medium heat and generously season your steaks with salt and pepper. If you're cooking indoors, get a griddle pan hot over a medium–high heat.

Lay those awesome hunks of meat on the grill or griddle and get cooking. If you're outdoors, keep them moving, watch out for fat fires and make sure you get that fat dancing! You want to cook your steaks to medium rare (about 6–8 minutes, keep turning and moving) – use a temperature probe to make sure it is perfectly cooked (check temperatures on page 16). Then take those cow slices off the heat and rest in a warm place for at least 5 minutes.

While the steaks are resting, get your chips cooking (see page 160). At the same time, put a cast-iron frying pan on the grill or over a high heat on the hob and get it red hot... I mean really red hot like your mum! Throw your butter into the pan, then just before the butter really starts to burn, chuck in the saffron and prawns. Keep them moving so they get a nice colour and look bright and tasty. After about 1 minute, add the salt, lemon and thyme leaves. Take off the heat and rest for a minute while you toast your buns.

Slice the beautiful steak so you have enough for you and all your mates. Place a layer of Beard Hair Chips on the bottom bun, followed by slices of steak. Top with those almighty prawns and finally the bun lid. You're welcome!

# LAMB RIB BURGER

I could marry this burger if it was legal! Seriously, this is the best-tasting meat ever and that's because of the lamb fat that surrounds it. A couple of years ago, the food critic Giles Coren and I travelled to Brazil on the Uruguay border to see where the gauchos raise the pure Black Angus cattle for the European beef market. Before we went cattle herding, we had coffee in the farmhouse. In front of the open hearth there were four long skewers with lamb ribs and belly slowly cooking, and a huge pool of lamb fat collecting on the stone floor. I wanted to dive straight into that pool of tastiness. The gaucho slid the meat onto a chopping board and we ate and ate and smiled and ate some more. Up there in the top 10 best things I've ever tasted. Here's my version of that delicious lamb, but in a burger. Way easier to eat!

---

🔪 **MAKES 4 BURGERS**

🍸 **OUTDOORS** Kettle-style grill with a lid, half & half technique

🍱 **INDOORS** Oven, plus griddle pan on the hob (stovetop)

---

1 rack of lamb ribs with breast attached
Chilli flakes (crushed chili pepper)
4 soft white buns
Sea salt and black pepper

### PINEAPPLE SALSA

1 pineapple, cut into steaks
12 cherry tomatoes, quartered
Zest and juice of 2 limes
1 medium red onion, finely chopped
Bunch of coriander (cilantro), chopped (stalks and all)
1 red chilli, deseeded and finely chopped

Get your lamb ribs out of the fridge at least an hour before you want to cook. Preheat your oven to 220°C (425°F/gas mark 7). If you're using the outdoor grill, get it up to the same temperature – nice and hot! Lightly score the lamb fat with a sharp knife, and season the joint with salt and chilli flakes.

Roast your lamb straight on a rack in the oven or right on the grill over direct heat, so the fat drips down and doesn't suffocate the meat. Cook for 20 minutes, then drop the heat to 135°C (275°F/gas mark 1). You'll need to cover with foil for both indoors and outdoors (put the lid on outdoors, too). Slow-cook for another 1½ hours.

While the lamb is cooking, get the pineapple salsa made. You need a high heat, so if you're cooking outside, do it in the first 20 minutes of the lamb cook. Inside, use a griddle pan in your own time. Grill the pineapple steaks until you have a nice char. Set them aside to cool, then dice.

Chuck the chopped pineapple into a bowl with all the other salsa ingredients, season with salt and pepper and mix well. Set aside for the main event.

*Recipe continues...*

*Recipe continued from page 128.*

After 1½ hours, remove the foil and lid, and see where you are at with the lamb cook. The meat should be pulling away from the bones and feel quite tender to the touch.

Continue cooking without foil until you've got a nice crisp on the outside. That crunchy savoury more-ish lamb fat will be the single best taste you'll have had since the first time you had a pork scratching in a sunny beer garden with a lovely pint of pilsner.

Let the lamb ribs rest for 5 minutes but not much longer – you do not want to bite into lukewarm or cold fat, it needs to be hot and crispy. Remove all the bones and slice the lamb ribs into bite-size morsels of pure lamb fat heaven. Oh gosh, I wanna cook this right now. So jealous of your burger!

Toast your buns (griddle pan or direct heat) and begin the build. If you wanna go a bit gnarly, dip the soft insides of the bun halves into the lamb fat before toasting. Naughty deliciousness!

Here's the build: bottom bun, lamb rib meat, salsa, love – but don't get lost in your creation, you still need to put the top bun on and eat! – top bun, eat!

# EXTRA BEEFY BEEF CHEEK BURGER

Beef cheeks are something I love cooking and they always turn up when you don't expect them. One time was when T-Bone turned up at my door two and a half hours early, holding a pack of half-frozen beef cheeks he'd found in his parents' freezer, with a big smile on his face, blabbering 'I woke up at 3am with an epiphany! Braised beef cheek and roasted sprout burger.' This seriously happened on the very last day of the book shoot. True story. And here it is.

---

🔪 **MAKES 2 BURGERS**

🍴 **OUTDOORS** Half & half technique, with a lidded casserole and large frying pan

🍳 **INDOORS** Oven, plus a lidded casserole and frying pan

---

## BEEF CHEEKS

200g (7oz/1⅔ cup) plain
   (all-purpose) flour
2 beef cheeks
Light olive oil or vegetable oil,
   for frying
2 carrots, diced
2 celery sticks, diced
1 onion, diced
1 whole garlic bulb, sliced in half
2 anchovies in oil, chopped
2 bay leaves
2 rosemary sprigs
250ml (9fl oz/generous 1 cup)
   red wine
200g (7oz/scant 1 cup) passata
1 litre (35fl oz/4¼ cups) beef stock
1 tbsp English mustard
2 star anise
4 cloves
Sea salt and black pepper

## SPROUTS

500g (1lb 2oz) brussels sprouts,
   halved
1 tbsp olive oil
100g (3½oz) bacon lardons
25g (¾oz) butter
Squeeze of lemon juice

## TO SERVE

2 brioche buns
Parsnip Ketchup (page 164)

Preheat your oven to 150°C (300°F/gas mark 2) or get a gentle fire going on your outdoor grill.

Tip your flour into a shallow bowl or small roasting tin (pan) and heavily season with salt and pepper. Gently press the beef cheeks in the flour until they are lightly coated.

Heat some oil in a casserole over a medium heat on the hob (or over the direct heat on the grill), add the beef cheeks and brown them off on all sides. Remove the cheeks from the pan and set aside on a plate, then throw all the veg, anchovies, bay leaves and rosemary into the casserole. Fry off until golden brown, then put the beef cheeks back in, along with the wine, passata, stock, mustard, star anise and cloves. Bring up to the boil and then place in the oven or on the grill (with the lid) for 3–4 hours, until the beef is tender.

When the cheeks are tender, remove from the pan and set aside on a plate. Strain the cooking liquor into another pan and set over a gentle heat to reduce, until thick and shiny (about 15 minutes), discarding the star anise and cloves. When the sauce has reduced, put the beef cheeks back in and leave to rest until you are ready to build that amazeballs burger!

While the sauce is reducing, boil the sprouts for 5 minutes in salted water, then plunge in a bowl of cold water. When cool, drain them on paper towels. Add the olive oil to a large frying pan and fry the bacon lardons until crispy. Add in the butter and sprouts. Fry until rich and awesome, then season with a squeeze of lemon juice and some salt and pepper.

Toast your buns and layer up that beef cheek you have given so much love to. Start with the bottom bun, followed by the sprouts, beefy beef cheek, some sauce, more sauce and a bit more sauce, and some more sauce after that, heck, just have a bath in it! Finish with some tangy Parsnip Ketchup. Careful when you eat this, as you might just love yourself so much you will change your name to the Duke of Dang Diddly Ball Bags.

# L'AMERICAIN (IT'S ACTUALLY A FRENCH INVENTION)

I discovered this tasty treat while snowboarding in the French Alps, in between my mission to eat as many tartiflettes as possible. The fast-food joints sometimes have this on the menu. Their version involves two grilled steak hachés, chips and burger sauce. Yes, there is a sauce dedicated to burgers. I reckon this version is slightly (WAY) better.

🔪 **SERVES 4 (OR 2 IF YOU'RE SUPER HUNGRY)**

🍴 **OUTDOORS** Half & half technique, with a frying pan for the onions; not recommended for the chips

🗄 **INDOORS** Oven, plus frying pan and griddle pan on the hob (stovetop), plus deep-fat fryer or deep saucepan

1 × 300g (10½oz) bavette steak
(other steaks will still rock)
1 medium French stick
Sea salt and black pepper
Secret Burger Sauce (page 164)

## CHIPS

4 large baking potatoes
Vegetable oil, for deep-fat frying
(at least 2 litres/3½ pints)

## ONIONS

1 tbsp butter, for frying
1 medium onion, sliced
250ml (9fl oz/generous 1 cup)
white wine or génépi if you
can get it

First, let's get those chips rocking. The best chips come from baked potatoes. It's pretty much like doing a twice-cooked chip! Make them the day before, as the potatoes need to cool completely before deep-frying.

Preheat the oven to 180°C (350°F/gas mark 4). Bake your potatoes for 45–60 minutes. Pull them out and let them cool.

When it comes to the actual cooking, make sure you get that steak out of the fridge an hour beforehand. No one likes a cold steak, especially your grill or griddle pan. It's a muscle and it needs to relax before it meets the heat.

While the steak is relaxing, slice the cooled potatoes into skinny chips, like classic fries.

Burger sauce time! Really carefully slam all the sauce ingredients into a bowl and scream, 'Good game, son!' Mix together with a baseball bat or spoon. I prefer a spoon, my 11-year-old prefers the baseball bat or T-Bone's machete. That didn't come out right.

L'oignon moment! Place the butter in a frying pan set over the direct heat on the grill or on a low to medium heat on the hob. When the butter has melted, add the onion. Cook until the onion goes translucent – about 5 minutes – then throw in the splash of white wine or génépi and continue cooking for a few more minutes until golden. Turn off the heat but keep in the pan so they stay warm for the build.

Season the steak with salt and place on the grill over direct heat, or in a griddle pan over a medium to high heat on the hob. Move the steak around and get all sides seared – you want to create a nice crust on the outside. Don't go too far as the outside can burn and taste bitter. I like to serve steak medium to medium rare. Use a temperature probe to see if the steak is cooked (check the internal meat temperatures on page 16) – then remove. Crack some pepper on it and keep warm.

Now for the chips. Pour the oil into a large, deep saucepan (or you can use a deep-fat fryer), set it over a high heat and get that oil hot. Once the temperature reaches 180°C (350°F), you are good to fry. Use a temperature probe to check the oil temperature – not your finger like T-Bone once did. Silly rabbit! Carefully cast your chips into the super-hot oil. Cook in batches for 1–2 minutes until golden brown and crispy, then remove with a slotted spoon onto a paper towel. Season with salt and pepper.

Now assembly time!

Slice the French stick lengthways. Then cut it into 4 or 2 depending on how greedy you are. Toast the bread by placing it soft side down on your grill or in the pan over a hot heat. Once golden and toasted, pull them off to begin construction.

Lay the bottom part of the French stick out. Thinly slice the steak against the grain. Then roll the meat around in the resting juices and sprinkle with salt. Get that meat seasoned. Place the chips onto the toasted bread. The more the merrier! Throw some sliced steak over your shoulder and onto the chips. How stoked is your dog? All the meat for Rambler (other dog names are available)! Sorry about the steak all over your kitchen. Alternatively, gently place the steak onto the chips. Versez délicatement les oignons sur la viande (spoon the onions onto the steak). Generously slather the top bun with the Burger Sauce and slap it on top of this super-duper triply next-level creation.

And mangez! That's French for eat!

# CRUNCHY PORK BURGER WITH APPLE SLAW

Nothing goes together better than pork and apple – apart from maybe pork scratchings and beer. So, in this case, feel free to drink beer while eating this insane beast cos you are gonna top the burger with the most delicious, naughty, savoury snack ever invented.

---

🔪 **MAKES 4 BURGERS**

🍖 **OUTDOORS** Half & half technique

🍳 **INDOORS** Griddle pan on the hob (stovetop)

---

400g (14oz) pork mince (ground pork), a fatty shoulder cut works well, or leg meat
1 tbsp very finely chopped rosemary leaves
1 tbsp chopped sage leaves
1 tsp finely chopped thyme leaves
Pinch of grated nutmeg
4 seeded burger buns
1 x packet pork scratchings
Sea salt and black pepper

## APPLE SLAW

1 apple, cored and cut into matchsticks
¼ small white cabbage, thinly sliced
1 small red onion, thinly sliced
4 radishes, thinly sliced
1 tbsp mayonnaise
1 tsp English mustard
1 tsp cider vinegar

First, make your slaw by mixing all the ingredients together in a bowl, like some sort of slaw god, you slaw god you! Set aside.

Place the pork mince, herbs and nutmeg in a large bowl or on a chopping board and mix well. Next, divide the herby porky mince into four balls and flatten into lovely looking patties.

Get your grill nice and hot, or set your griddle pan over a medium heat on the hob. Season your patties with salt and pepper, then get cooking.

If you're cooking outdoors, the meat might stick to the grill – remember, the grill will release the meat when it's ready. Cook for 1–2 minutes, then flip, and repeat the process until they are almost done. Keep grilling and flipping until you create a nice golden crust – about 10–12 minutes. Use a temperature probe to make sure the burger is perfectly cooked – check the internal meat temperatures on page 16, then remove your burgers and keep warm.

Now toast your buns and get ready for the build!

Lay out the bottom bun and place that hot slab of porky herby radeliciousness on it, then top with the slaw. Finish with some crushed-up pork scratchings and finally the top bun. Gosh dang it! I need a cold beer right now just thinking of this next-level porktastic treat.

Now play Black Sabbath's 'War Pigs' as loud as your system – or the landlord – will allow it!

Feast on said beast!

# CHICKEN TENDERS WAFFLE BURGER

Ever wonder what to do with the little piece of awesome flesh that is attached to the underside of every chicken breast? Well, these are often known as chicken tenders or mini-fillets and they are said to be more tender and tasty than the main meat. In this recipe, you are going to deep-fry these bad boys and serve them with the only thing decadent enough to handle these tasty treats... waffles. We've got a life-changing recipe for the best waffles ever – just head to the next page.

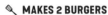 **MAKES 2 BURGERS**

🍴 **OUTDOORS** Not recommended

🔥 **INDOORS** Frying pan on the hob (stovetop), plus deep-fat fryer or deep saucepan

Vegetable oil, for deep-fat frying (at least 2 litres/3½ pints)
150g (5½oz/1¼ cups) plain (all-purpose) flour
2 eggs, beaten
150g (5½oz) panko breadcrumbs
4 medium-large chicken tenders
4 smoked streaky bacon rashers (slices)
100ml (3½fl oz/scant ½ cup) maple syrup
1 tsp mustard seeds
4 square waffles (either freshly made, page 144, or shop-bought)
¼ iceberg lettuce, shredded
2 pickles, sliced
2 tbsp Heavy Metal Black Garlic Mayo (page 92)
Sea salt and black pepper

Pour the oil into a large, deep saucepan (or you can use a deep-fat fryer), set it over a high heat and get that oil hot. Once the temperature reaches 180°C (350°F), you are good to fry.

Place the flour, egg and breadcrumbs into three separate shallow bowls or trays. Season the chicken, then dip and coat each chicken tender in the flour, then the egg and finally the breadcrumbs, and rest on a tray.

When the fryer is hot enough, carefully drop each chicken tender into the oil and deep-fry until fully cooked and golden brown – about 6–8 minutes. Drain on paper towels.

While the chicken is cooking, fry the bacon in a dry frying pan until really crispy and awesome!

Put the maple syrup into a small pan and add the mustard seeds. Heat up gently over a low heat on the hob until hot, then leave to cool.

Heat up your waffles, either in a toaster or over the grill if you're part-cooking outdoors. Now get ready to build your waffle tower!

Pick two waffles to be your bottoms, and add some lettuce, two chicken tenders and two slices of bacon. On the top waffles, slap on some garlic mayo and top with pickle slices. Finally, drizzle the cooled mustard maple syrup all over the bacon, bang on the top waffle and crack on!

# BEST WAFFLE IN THE HISTORY OF EVOLUTION (UNTIL NOW, BUT PROBABLY FOREVER)

The waffle is the best invention ever! Apart from Iron Maiden, Kings of Leon and Aretha Franklin (RIP you lovely woman). All ages love 'em. If you are a parent, dang, this is the go-to recipe. And they go great with Chicken Tenders (page 143). Special thanks to Billie Buns for her help with this recipe. Billie is the better half of David Wright (our baker).

 **MAKES ABOUT 20**

 **OUTDOORS** Not recommended

 **INDOORS** Waffle maker

215g (7½oz/1¾ cups) plain (all-purpose) flour
70g (2½oz/½ cup) cornflour (cornstarch)
1 tsp baking powder
½ tsp bicarbonate of soda (baking soda)
½ tsp fine sea salt
360ml (12fl oz/1½ cups) buttermilk (if you don't have buttermilk, you could add 1½ tsp lemon juice to the same quantity of full-fat (whole) milk and leave to curdle)
120ml (4fl oz/½ cup) water
90ml (3fl oz/generous ⅓ cup) vegetable oil
2 eggs, separated
40g (1½ oz/scant ¼ cup) caster (superfine) sugar

Preheat the oven to 180°C (350°F/gas mark 4). And also preheat your waffle maker.

Mix all of the dry ingredients (except the sugar) together in a bowl and make a well in the centre. In a bowl, mix all of the wet ingredients together, apart from the egg whites, until well combined.

Whisk the egg whites until soft peaks form. Add the sugar and whip until you have stiff peaks.

Fold the buttermilk mixture into the dry mixture, stirring until just combined – lumps are good! Then, gently fold in the egg whites.

In batches, pour the batter into a waffle maker set to a medium heat and cook until done and perfectly golden – about 5 minutes, or as per the manufacturer's instructions.

Transfer to a baking sheet in the oven to keep warm and crisp up, while you continue making more waffles until all the batter is used up.

# ROASTED PORK BELLY BURGER

There is nothing like a good old Sunday pub lunch of roasted pork belly, apple sauce, mash and cabbage – even better after a round of pork scratchings and a couple of pints of ale. And even better in a burger!

---

🔪 **MAKES 4 BURGERS**

🍖 **OUTDOORS** Kettle-style grill with lid or hot smoker

🍴 **INDOORS** Oven, plus saucepans on the hob (stovetop)

You will also need a roasting tin (pan)

---

1.2kg (2lb 10oz) pork belly, skin on, un-scored
4 seeded burger buns
1 jar sauerkraut
Sea salt and black pepper
Table salt

### APPLE SAUCE
2 eating apples, peeled and diced
2 tbsp apple juice
1 tsp butter
Pinch of salt

### MASH
2–3 medium floury potatoes, peeled and cubed
50g (1¾oz) butter
1 tbsp milk

Preheat the oven to 220°C (425°F/gas mark 7) or get your coals cooking with a large indirect side.

Remove the skin from the pork belly and set aside. Lightly score the fat remaining on the belly and season with salt and pepper. Stick it in a roasting tin (pan) and put it in the oven. After 25 minutes, lower the temperature to 160°C (310°F/gas mark 2½) and roast for another 2 hours. If you're cooking outside, make sure the cooker is really hot (220°C /425°F). Then place the pork above indirect heat, with a drip pan underneath the grill to collect the juices and fat. After 25 minutes, use the pinwheels to suffocate the airflow and bring the temperature inside the cooker to 160°C (310°F) for the rest of the cook.

While the pork is roasting, score the whole pork skin and place it on a baking sheet. Stick it in the sink and pour a full kettle of boiling water over the skin. Then leave the skin on a cooling rack to dry out for a couple of hours.

Next, make the apple sauce. Chuck the diced apple in a saucepan along with the apple juice, butter and salt. Add in half a glass of water and bring to the boil. Next, lower the heat and gently simmer for 15–20 minutes, stirring occasionally until thick and creamy. Set aside to cool.

When the pork belly is cooked, remove it from the oven and turn the oven up to 230°C (450°F/gas mark 8). The pork skin should have dried out by now. Rub table salt all over the skin, massaging it into the score lines. Place the skin on a rack in the oven and roast for 20–30 minutes until the top blisters up. Remove and cool, until crispy.

Now it's mash time! Bring a medium saucepan full of water to the boil and drop the chunked spuds in.

Cook for 15 minutes or until the potatoes are soft enough to mash. Drain and put them back into the pan. Add the butter and milk, and season with salt and pepper. Mash until smooth and creamy.

When everything is ready, slice that rambunctious pork into eight solid slices. Toast your buns, then layer up the mash, belly slices, sauerkraut, apple sauce and pork scratchings.

# LAMB CHORIZO BURGER WITH APRICOT SALSA

Get ready to jump on the food party train when creating this beautiful gift to humankind. First off, it's got lamb fat, and I could marry lamb fat if it was allowed. Saying that, I'm an ordained member of the Spiritual Humanist clergy. Maybe I could perform the wedding myself. 'Do you, DJ BBQ, take this lamb fat, to love and to hold, to cherish and to devour?' DJ BBQ: 'I do.' But back to the burger…

---

✎ **MAKES 4 BURGERS**

🍖 **OUTDOORS** Half & half technique

🍳 **INDOORS** Griddle pan on the hob (stovetop)

---

200g (7 oz) cooking chorizo, skinned and chopped
500g (1lb 2oz) lamb shoulder, minced (ground)
4 brioche burger buns
4 tbsp Smoked Garlic Mayo (page 95), optional

**SALSA**

3 ripe, fresh apricots, chopped
1 medium red onion, finely chopped
1 tbsp chopped or torn mint leaves
Juice of ½ lemon
Pinch of sugar
Pinch of chilli flakes (crushed chili pepper)
Sea salt and black pepper

Evenly mix the chopped chorizo into the lamb mince. Divide the mix into four balls and flatten them into patties a little bit larger than the buns, as you will get shrinkage as the fats render. You don't need to season these burgers, because of the salty chorizo in the mix.

When your patties are ready, set them aside while your grill is getting fired up! If you're cooking indoors, set a griddle pan over a medium to high heat on the hob.

Now let's make the salsa. Combine all the salsa ingredients in a bowl. Season to taste. Remember, the chorizo is quite salty so take it easy.

When the grill is rocking or the griddle hot, get the patties over direct heat or into the pan. If you're cooking outdoors, you will get some flare-ups because of the fat content in the chorizo and the lamb mince, but you've got your indirect heat goof-proof zone to go to if things get out of hand.

Grill or griddle until you have a lovely crust on the outside and the patties are cooked nicely throughout (about 5 minutes per side).

Toast your buns, then get ready to create a mouth party sensation. I am so excited for your taste buds right now! You probably don't believe me – I could be sleeping! – but I'm always excited… and I don't sleep much. Anyway!

Sometimes, I start by slathering Smoked Garlic Mayo on the bottom bun, but this is optional. Then add the burger, top with your freshly made apricot salsa and enjoy.

# CHICKEN-FRIED CHICKEN BURGER

This recipe was donated by our good friend, Scott Hallsworth. Scott was the head chef of Nobu for six years and currently owns and runs Freak Scene in London. I hosted a live fire demo with Scott last autumn and asked him, 'Did you name your restaurant after the Dinosaur Jr. song, Freak Scene?' He responded, 'Yeah, I did' in his rad Aussie accent. I then asked, 'Are you going to see them next month when they play London?' Scott was perplexed, he had no idea they were touring. I immediately called my son and told him that he couldn't bring a friend and gave that ticket to Scott. Sorry, Blue. A ticket for a recipe. That's how it works! Ha. The gig was rad! As is this chicken literally fried in chicken. You can order Chicken-fried Chicken without the bun at his restaurant every day. Or you can make it yourself. Whoohoooooo! Note, the chicken takes a good bit of prep. It needs marinating and then chilling and a fair amount of prep. So start this recipe well in advance – it's worth it!

 **MAKES 4 BURGERS**

 **OUTDOORS** Not recommended

 **INDOORS** Oven, plus deep saucepan on the hob (stovetop)

You'll also need a blender

## MARINADE

40g (1½oz) garlic, peeled and roughly chopped
3 lemongrass sticks, top third discarded, roughly chopped
20g (¾oz) ginger, peeled and roughly chopped
30g (1oz) coriander (cilantro) roots and stems (reserve leaves for later), roughly chopped
3 large red chillies, roughly chopped
45ml (1½fl oz/3 tbsp) vegetable oil
20g (¾oz/1 tbsp) sea salt

First, make the marinade for the chicken. Chuck all the ingredients into a blender and blitz on a high speed until smooth.

Massage the marinade paste into the chicken legs. Place the chicken into a non-metallic dish and pour in any remaining marinade. Cover with cling film (plastic wrap) and refrigerate for 12 hours.

Preheat your oven to 140°C (285°F/gas mark 1). Rinse the marinade off the chicken legs and leave them to drain in a colander for at least 10 minutes. Then place the chicken legs in a roasting tin (pan) that is just big enough to hold the legs snugly.

Put the duck fat in a saucepan over a medium heat on the hob and warm through until it's liquid, then pour it over the chicken legs. The legs should be fully submerged. Cover the tin with foil and cook in the oven for 2 hours.

After 2 hours, take it out of the oven, carefully remove the foil and gently test a chicken leg.

*Ingredients and recipe continue...*

## CHICKEN

4 corn-fed chicken legs (leg
and thigh attached, bone in)
1.5 litres (2½ pints/6⅓ cups)
duck fat
2 litres (3½ pints) chicken fat

## AMAZU PICKLED CUCUMBER

200ml (7fl oz/generous ¾ cup)
Japanese rice vinegar
130g (4½oz/⅔ cup) caster
(superfine) sugar
12g (½oz/2½ tsp) table salt
1 large cucumber, skin on, thinly
sliced on a mandolin

## PEANUT SOY SAUCE

200g (7oz) unsalted peanuts,
roasted and partially crushed
(in a tea towel with a rolling pin,
or use a pestle and mortar)
250ml (9fl oz/generous 1 cup)
kecap manis (not technically
a soy sauce, but sometimes
referred to sweet soy sauce)
1 or 2 dried red chillies, crushed
up into flakes – add more or
less, depending on your chilli
threshold!

## TO SERVE

4 buns
Mayonnaise
4 sprigs of coriander (cilantro)
1 or 2 long green chillies, sliced
Handful of mizuna leaves
(optional)

*Recipe continued from page 150.*

You want the flesh to fall away super-easily – but be careful, because if you try to pick up a leg, it may even just fall apart! You want to let it cool in the fat for at least a couple of hours before attempting to fry it. The best thing to do is chill it in the fridge for a few hours or overnight.

Meanwhile, you can make the pickled cucumber. Gently heat the rice vinegar, sugar and salt in a pan until the sugar and salt have dissolved. Be careful not to bring this to the boil – boiling ruins the delicate nuances of a good-quality vinegar. You've now got what is referred to in Japanese cuisine as amazu, a highly versatile pickling solution (seriously awesome when used on mackerel). Allow it to cool to room temperature, then pour it over your cucumber slices and leave to steep for a good hour before using. You could also keep these beauties refrigerated overnight but it is best when they are freshly pickled.

For the peanut soy, mix all the ingredients together and store at room temperature. It keeps indefinitely, but it is way better when freshly mixed and served right away.

When you are ready to cook your chicken, put the 2 litres of chicken fat in a deep saucepan over a medium to high heat on the hob. When the fat reaches 180°C (350°F), you are good to fry!

Wipe off any excess fat and chicken jelly from your confit legs and place one leg at a time into the hot fat. Fry for about 4–5 minutes or until the skin is beautifully bronzed. Remove and drain on paper towels, then gently pull the bones away from the meat – they will slip away easily.

Now, build! Add a squirt of mayo to the bun base, lay your confit chicken down, top with a spoonful of peanut soy, a slice of pickled cucumber, a sprig of coriander and as much green chilli as you can handle. If you feel guilty about the lack of healthiness, add a handful of mizuna leaves. And enjoy – you have earned this!

# WEST VIRGINIA BURGER

During my time at the University of Maryland, I dated a woman called Randi Stanko who went to the University of West Virginia. She would take me to a rad restaurant on campus that sold their fries with blue cheese dressing. I never liked blue cheese dressing, I was more of an Italian or ranch guy. But for some strange reason, it works really well with a savoury crunchy deep-fried potatoey thing. The more joints I frequented around Morgantown, West Virginia, the more I saw 'Fries and Blue' on the menu. It's like their standard thing. Kinda like mayo on chips in Amsterdam. I became addicted. I had finally broken through the blue cheese barrier!

---

🔪 **MAKES 4 BURGERS**

🍖 **OUTDOORS** Half & half technique; not recommended for the chips

📟 **INDOORS** Griddle pan and frying pan on the hob (stovetop)

You'll also need a deep-fat fryer or deep saucepan

---

Chips, any you like (pages 160–1)
500g (1lb 2oz) beef mince (ground beef)
100g (3½oz) mushrooms, sliced
1 tbsp butter, for frying
Splash of Worcestershire sauce
4 slices of burger cheese
4 burger buns
Sea salt and black pepper

**BLUE CHEESE DRESSING**
75g (2¾oz/⅔ cup) sour cream
½ tsp Dijon mustard
1 garlic clove, pulverized
1 tsp red wine vinegar
1 tbsp mayonnaise
40g (1½oz) blue cheese
1 tbsp lemon juice
Pinch of salt and pepper

First, make your chips – choose your favourite recipe from pages 160–1.

While that's in progress, make the blue cheese dressing. Combine all the ingredients together in a mixing bowl and stir until gloopily smooth. Of course, you can buy the dressing pre-made in a bottle. But if you do, your children and dog will hate you or at least think less of you. Actually, shop-bought blue cheese dressing is amazing. I love it! Hell, just do that. Skip this section.

Divide the beef mince into four balls and flatten them into beautiful patties a little bit larger than the buns – you'll get shrinkage as the fats render.

Get your grill nice and hot, or set your griddle pan over a high heat on the hob. Season your patties with salt and pepper, then get cooking. If you're cooking outdoors, the meat might stick to the grill – don't worry, relax, the grill will release the meat when it's ready. Cook for 1–2 minutes, then flip, and repeat the process until they are almost done.

Meanwhile, cook the sliced mushrooms in the butter in a frying pan over a low to medium heat. Splash some Worcestershire sauce into the mix. Cook until soft – about 5 minutes.

These burgers are best served medium rare to medium. When they're almost cooked – after about 6 minutes – add the cheese slices on top of each burger. You can forget the burger cheese if you like – it is an indulgence, as you already have

the blue cheese rocking in the dressing. But I like to go the whole hog... except with cow, so, go the whole cow!

Use a temperature probe to make sure the burger is perfectly cooked – check the internal meat temperatures on page 16 – then remove your burgers and keep warm while you toast your buns and finish off the chips.

Now, let's put this thang together. Bottom bun followed by cheesy patty, followed by mushrooms and a good portion of chips. Now make it rain blue cheese dressing. Go with a full-on avalanche of tangy gooey goodness. Oh goodness, dag nabbit, I want this super-savoury tangy burger right now! There will be loads of leftover chips, so use them as a snack. Dip 'em in that sauce!

# CHIPS, FRIES & CONDIMENTS

# DJ BBQ CHIPS SELECTION BOX OF FUN

Burgers need chips – fried and potatoey goodness. The world's lust for the fried potato in any form is relentless and we love them so much we couldn't resist doing them at festivals – and in this book!

---

🍴 **EACH RECIPE MAKES ENOUGH FOR AT LEAST 4**

🍖 **OUTDOORS** Not recommended

🍳 **INDOORS** Deep-fat fryer, or deep saucepan on the hob (stovetop), plus oven for some recipes

---

# DJ BBQ CHIPS

These are our go-to chips for most dishes and we have served them many times at festivals. So so so crunchy!

4 large baking potatoes
Vegetable oil, for deep-fat frying
    (at least 2 litres/3½ pints)
Sea salt and black pepper

---

Preheat your oven to 180°C (350°F/gas mark 4). Or if you're cooking outside, get your grill nice and hot.

Bake your potatoes whole for 45 minutes–1 hour, until tender. Or, for smoky vibes, cook these over indirect heat on the grill, for 1–1½ hours, depending on the size of the potato. You can throw some wood on the coals for the extra smoky flavour.

Leave the potatoes to cool for 1 hour (or overnight).

Pour the oil into a large deep saucepan (or you can use a deep-fat fryer), set it over a high heat and get that oil hot. Once the temperature reaches 180°C (350°F), you are good to fry.

Cut the potatoes into wedges and deep-fry for 1–2 minutes until golden brown. Remove onto some paper towels to drain, and season with salt and pepper.

# BEARD HAIR CHIPS

If you ever wondered what chips would be like if they were made in homage to T-Bone's beard hair (!), well... this is the answer! A supreme taste sensation!

2 baking potatoes
Vegetable oil, for deep-fat frying
    (at least 2 litres/3½ pints)
Sea salt and black pepper

---

You need a Japanese-style mandolin with a fine julienne cutter. Be careful as mandolins can hurt if you get it wrong so use a guard!

Peel the potatoes and carefully slice them using the fine julienne cutter on the mandolin. When you have got your chips, soak them in cold water for 1 hour.

Pour the oil into a large deep saucepan (or you can use a deep-fat fryer), set it over a high heat and get that oil hot. Once the temperature reaches 180°C (350°F), you are good to fry.

When the oil is hot, drain your chips well on paper towels. Deep-fry for a couple of minutes until golden brown, drain again on clean paper towels, and season with salt and pepper.

# SWEET POTATO CHIPS

Everyone loves chips. But sweet potato chips are the younger rad cousin that everyone's afraid to make but happy to order at a restaurant. They aren't as easy to make as their more famous family member, but this recipe will sort you right out.

500g (1lb 2oz) sweet potatoes, peeled and cut into chips
Vegetable oil, for deep-fat frying (at least 2 litres/3½ pints)
200g (7oz/1¾ cups) gluten-free flour
2 tbsp paprika
1 tbsp sea salt
Rosemary leaves, finely chopped, to finish

---

Soak the raw sweet potato chips in a bowl of cold water for 50 minutes.

Pour the oil into a large deep saucepan (or you can use a deep-fat fryer), set it over a high heat and get that oil hot. Once the temperature reaches 170°C (325°F), you are good to fry.

Combine the flour, paprika and salt in a mixing bowl. Place a handful of chips into the bowl and evenly coat with the flour mix.

When the oil is hot, place the coated chips into the frying basket and slowly lower into the oil. Deep-fry for 5–6 minutes until golden and crispy.

Remove and drain on a paper towel. Repeat in batches until all the chips have been cooked, then season them with the rosemary and more sea salt.

Boom! Good luck explaining to your friends how you were able to make restaurant-style sweet potato chips. They will be astounded by your awesomeness.

# SKINNY FRIES

These fries are even crispier than the big DJ BBQ Chips as they have more surface area. Great with all burgers!

4 large baking potatoes
Vegetable oil, for deep-fat frying (at least 2 litres/3½ pints)
Sea salt and black pepper

---

Preheat your oven to 180°C (350°F/gas mark 4). Or if you're cooking outside, get your grill nice and hot. Bake your potatoes whole for 45 minutes–1 hour, in the oven. Or cook these over indirect heat on the grill, for 1–1½ hours, depending on the size of the potato. Leave to cool for 1 hour (or overnight).

Pour the oil into a large deep saucepan (or you can use a deep-fat fryer), set it over a high heat and get that oil hot. Once the temperature reaches 180°C (350°F), you are good to fry.

Cut the potatoes into thin fries and deep-fry for 1–2 minutes until golden brown. Remove onto some paper towels to drain, and season with salt and pepper.

# DJ BBQ'S HOT SAUCE OF RADNESS

During a damn-hot Jimmy's Festival one year, we got a new chef in to help T-Bone as he was a bit tired after fire-roasting 11 whole beef legs the year before! His name was Sam Jones, a generally hungover ex-poker-playing chalet chef from Cheltenham, who doesn't get up till after 2pm on work days! He eventually turned up and we tasked him with making a DJ BBQ hot sauce. He grabbed the leftover Mix of Rad rub (that we use in our pulled pork) and then grabbed anything else he could lay his hands on from our larder. After six hours and a lot of White Russians, the DJ BBQ's Hot Sauce of Radness was born!

---

🔪 **SERVES 10**

🍸 **OUTDOORS** Half & half technique, with a frying pan

🔥 **INDOORS** Frying pan on the hob (stovetop)

---

6 tbsp Mix of Rad (see below)
4 tbsp cola
2 tbsp apple juice
2 tbsp cider vinegar
2 tbsp ketchup
1 tbsp Dijon mustard
1 tbsp Worcestershire sauce
1 tbsp brown sugar
1 tbsp chilli powder

**MIX OF RAD**
2 tbsp brown sugar
1 heaped tbsp flaked sea salt
1 tbsp coarse ground black pepper
1 tbsp ground cumin
1 tbsp ground coriander
1 tbsp onion granules
1 tbsp garlic granules
½ tsp mustard powder
½ tsp chilli powder
½ tsp chilli flakes (crushed chili pepper)

First, make the Mix of Rad spice mix by throwing all the ingredients in a bowl and stirring until thoroughly combined.

(Keep what you don't use in this recipe for any other meat you need to throw on your grill.)

Place all the ingredients for the hot sauce in a cast-iron frying pan, stir everything together and set over a medium heat (either on the grill or on the hob). Let it bubble away until thick and hot.

At this point, you can add 100g (3½oz) butter to the pan to turn this into a buffalo sauce.

# PARSNIP KETCHUP

Parsnips have a wonderfully intense flavour and work so well with both sweet and sour flavours. This recipe involves both. Parsnip ketchup can be used instead of classic ketchup. It'll bring a whole new dimension of flavour to any beef or chicken burger. Heck, it'll even rock a pork burger. All the recipes in this book are open to swapping condiments around and this is one of the best to play with.

500g (1lb 2oz) parsnips, peeled and diced
150ml (5fl oz/⅔ cup) cider vinegar
100g (3½oz/½ cup) caster (superfine) sugar
50ml (1¾fl oz/scant ¼ cup) water
2 tbsp ground cumin
50ml (1¾fl oz/scant ¼ cup) olive oil, plus extra for the parsnips
Sea salt

Preheat the oven to 180°C (350°F/gas mark 4).

Place the diced parsnips into a roasting tin (pan). Drizzle on some olive oil and sprinkle with salt. Bake in the oven for about 25 minutes until golden. Remove and place in a large saucepan. Now add the rest of the ingredients, except for the olive oil, and bring to the boil. Simmer for 10 minutes. When it is cooked, all ya gotta do is add the olive oil and blend until smooth.

How's that for a next-level condiment?

# SECRET BURGER SAUCE

Have you ever seen one of Sean Penn's early films, *Fast Times at Ridgemont High*? Well, they divulge the classic burger sauce in there. One fast food joint makes its own, like I do, and the other uses Thousand Island Dressing, which is totally cool as well. It's super-quick, super-easy – you only need 3 ingredients – and super-secret (and simple). Shhhhhhhhhhhhhhhhhhhhhhhhhh.

225g (8oz/1 cup) mayonnaise
115g (4oz/½ cup) ketchup
1 gherkin (pickle), chopped

Mix everything together in a bowl and slather on your burger.

Don't tell anyone I told you.

Now, go make a burger and watch *Fast Times at Ridgemont High*. You are welcome!

# ÜBER TANGY COURGETTE RELISH

This recipe is so tangy it needs an umlaut (the two dots above the 'U'... creating a smiley face!). I relish the opportunity to share this tasty 'relish' recipe for your eating pleasure. It would be a good thing to cook 'to marrow'... sorry for all the puns! Let's get to the recipe before we start vegging out.

---

🍖 **OUTDOORS** Half & half technique, with a saucepan

📅 **INDOORS** Saucepan on the hob (stovetop)

---

1 tbsp butter
500g (1lb 2oz) courgettes (zucchini), sliced into matchsticks
1 green chilli, chopped (optional)
1 medium onion, grated
1 tbsp thyme leaves
225ml (7¾fl oz/scant 1 cup) cider vinegar
150g (5½oz/generous ¾ cup) brown sugar
1 tbsp English mustard
1 tbsp flaked sea salt

Set a saucepan over a high heat on the hob or over the direct heat on the grill. Chuck the butter in and, when it's melted, add in the courgette matchsticks and fry until slightly golden.

If you want to add some spice, throw in the optional chilli with the courgette. Add in the rest of the ingredients, bring to the boil, and let it simmer for 40 minutes. Leave to cool.

Store in the fridge in an airtight container. This should keep for at least a month.

# THANK YOU

Karen and Russ Taylor (Chris's folks who provided their home as a part-location)

Alfie, Ned, Choppy and Crosby (the dogs!)

Blue, Noah and Frasier (my three boys who will not stop growing. Who woulda thunk? You put good food in 'em and they grow like weeds)

Laura Curtis (the better half)

Sophie and Joshua (Chris's better half and kid)

Zena Alkayat (the best editor ever... gonna miss you, Z!)

David Loftus (the man, the myth, the legend and the good friend! Best photos in the world)

David Wright (voted best baker in the UK last year and the man behind the bread stuff)

Nathan Mills and the butchery team (Nath supplied the ground beef for the book)

David Foragey Fennings (right hand man and chef on all the shoot days)

Ramalamadingdong and Joey (Argentinian contingent)

Liz Norris (Sri Lankan Barbara Streisand and chef on shoot days)

Emily Lapworth (the rad designer with the gnarliest commute to work every day. Well, Emily wanted to live next to Stonehenge!)

Polly Webb-Wilson (rad props finder)

Sarah Chatwin (recipe editor of dreams)

Ruth Tewkesbury (publicity star)

Sarah Lavelle (the future editor)

Matt Williams (best charcoal maker ever)

Sam Jones (the giant chef slayer)

Martin Goodyear (driver of the food truck and maker of DJ BBQ merch)

Carl Brooks (DJ BBQ CREW muscle and front of house)

Bryony Morganna (front of house – check her amazing YouTube channel)

Johnny Boots (coolest dude we know)

Olivier Getdown (best party starter)

Toby Millage (DJ extraordinaire and the man responsible for the mosh pit at the *Fire Food* launch party. Oh, and best mate)

Elliot Chaffer (other best mate)

Marco and Adriano Sheppard (friends and chefs who soothe our weary souls)

Beach Bar Crew (favourite place in the world)

Scott Hallsworth and the Freak Scene family (ex-Nobu chef who worked on two recipes)

Dave and Ben and the Wingmans crew (best wings in the world and best chicken burger in the world)

Charlie at Walter Rose & Sons (our other amazing meat supplier)

Hellman's (world's best condiments that featured heavily in the book)

Rushton the veg man

Tom at Daily Fish

Sytchfarm and Hotdogsfortea (this wonderful husband and wife team crafted our plates and chopping boards)

Joe Preston

Renault for building the awesome catertainment truck and supplying my ride!

Andy Gregorek and the Gorilla Events lot

Bronski at Stetson Europe (cheers for the lids)

Netherton Foundry (the spun-iron pans featured in the book were crafted by this wonderful family)

Witloft (bad ass leather aprons featured in the book)

Risdon & Risdon (amazing canvas aprons featured in the book)

Edd Martin at Volcom (most fun dude in the world who hooked us up with amazing threads)

Matty, Ross and Will at Coalition Brewing (thanks for the suds, y'all)

Weber UK (our preferred cooker)

Pole and Hunt axes

Fingal Ferguson (really rad blades)/Blenheim Forge (super rad blades)/Joel Blacksmith (crazy ass blades)

Gransfors Bruks

Nick Weston (look out for the DJ BBQ vs Hunter Gather Cook events each spring)

Wayne Yates (Bafta-winning best mate)

Billie BUns (for her waffle knowledge)

Ruby (Mom) (for getting me in the kitchen)

Finally, Dad & Pam (the best parents ever)

# INDEX

**PUBLISHING DIRECTOR**
Sarah Lavelle

**COMMISSIONING EDITOR**
Zena Alkayat

**DRAGON SLAYER /
CO-RECIPE DEVELOPER**
Chris Taylor (T-Bone Chops)

**DESIGN AND ART DIRECTION**
Emily Lapworth

**PHOTOGRAPHER**
David Loftus

**PROPS STYLIST**
Polly Webb-Wilson

**ASSISTANT FOOD STYLIST**
Dave Fennings

**PRODUCTION DIRECTOR**
Vincent Smith

**PRODUCTION CONTROLLER**
Tom Moore

Published in 2019 by Quadrille,
an imprint of Hardie Grant Publishing

Quadrille
52–54 Southwark Street
London SE1 1UN
quadrille.com

Cataloguing in Publication Data: a catalogue record
for this book is available from the British Library.

Text © DJ BBQ (Christian Stevenson) 2019
Photography © David Loftus 2019
Design © Quadrille 2019

ISBN 978–1–78713–364–8

Reprinted in 2019
10 9 8 7 6 5 4 3 2

Printed in China

**DJ BBQ (AKA CHRISTIAN STEVENSON)**
is a live fire chef and a totally rad
personality in the world of BBQ. After
a successful broadcasting career
fronting shows for MTV, Channel 4
and Channel 5, he harnessed his
passion for cooking over fire and now
has his own YouTube channel with
more than 179k subscribers. DJ BBQ
stars in and hosts festivals including
Meatopia, The Big Feastival, Camp
Bestival, Grilltopia and The Big Grill.